INTRODUCTION

I am happy to have the opportunity to introduce you to this fine new book on duplicate bridge. Partly, this is because you could not possibly do better than to learn from Edgar Kaplan— a professional teacher and author as well as one of the most consistently successful tournament champions.

But my other reason is more selfish. Duplicate bridge is the fastest growing game in the country. Our American Contract Bridge League tournaments are twice the size they were three years ago, ten times the size they were in the 1950's. There are thousands of new duplicate clubs affiliated with the A.C.B.L.— it is a rare community which does not have its local master-point games. It is only natural for me to take pride in this magnificent burst of interest in the game I love and in the amazing growth of our organization.

Therefore, I am delighted that there is to be a mass-market book to bring the fun of duplicate to millions more bridge players. Having read this book, I can assure you of this: it will make a good duplicate player out of any rubber-bridge buff; and it will help make a Life Master out of any tournament enthusiast.

Alvin Landy
Executive Secretary,
American Contract Bridge League

DUPLICATE BRIDGE:
HOW TO PLAY, HOW TO WIN
BY EDGAR KAPLAN

BANTAM BOOKS
TORONTO · NEW YORK · LONDON

DUPLICATE BRIDGE: HOW TO PLAY, HOW TO WIN
A Bantam Book / published August 1966
2nd printing
3rd printing
4th printing

Library of Congress Catalog Card Number: 66–22421

Published simultaneously in the United States and Canada

Bantam Books are published by Bantam Books, Inc., a subsidiary
of Grosset & Dunlap, Inc. Its trade-mark, consisting of the words
"Bantam Books" and the portrayal of a bantam, is registered in the
United States Patent Office and in other countries. Marca Registrada.
Bantam Books, Inc., 271 Madison Avenue, New York, N. Y. 10016.

PRINTED IN THE UNITED STATES OF AMERICA

CONTENTS

FOREWORD

Have you ever played duplicate bridge? If you *are* a regular duplicate fan, you may have noticed that certain players in your game get surprisingly good results even though their card play and bidding are distinctly inferior to yours. Do you wonder why?

If you have never tried duplicate, it may be because of some vague feeling that you will be outclassed; that duplicate players are all experts. Nonsense! If you are a winning rubber-bridge player, your overall bridge game (your technique, your judgment) is probably superior to the average player's in a typical duplicate contest. However, the first few times that you play duplicate, you will do poorly. Why?

The answer to both "whys" above is that the scoring of duplicate makes it into a game sharply different from rubber bridge. The skills of card play are the same, but the bidding requires an entirely new set of tactics. And that is what this book is all about.

My assumption is that you are already a competent bridge player, and I will not try to improve your game. But competence is not enough to let you win at duplicate. You must suit your bidding tactics to the special requirements of the game. You must learn the tricks of the trade.

E.K.
New York City, 1966

I. DUPLICATE BRIDGE

The principal objective of "duplicate" is to eliminate from the game of bridge the single biggest luck factor: Who holds the cards? Each deal that you play is replayed, under identical conditions, at other tables. Your score is then compared with the results earned by those who held the same cards you did. This *comparison*, not your actual plus or minus, is what determines whether you do well or badly.

At rubber bridge, if you bid a vulnerable game and win all thirteen tricks on a deal in which your side has enough high cards to choke a hippopotamus, you end up with a profit. The opponents may sneer, but meanwhile you are smugly totting up the rubber. At duplicate, though, your paltry game is compared to the slams that others have bid and made with your cards, and you will receive the disastrous score that you deserve. Similarly, you can earn a triumphant score at duplicate by being set "only" 500 on an unlucky deal in which everyone else who holds your cards is in much deeper trouble. At rubber bridge, triumphs like this lead you straight to the poorhouse.

SCORING

In order for the comparisons to be fair, each deal at duplicate is scored as a separate unit (rather than as part of a series of hands such as a rubber, in which the results of *previous* deals can affect the scoring of the present one). There are never partial scores held over from earlier hands. All the conditions of play—who is dealer, which side is vulnerable—are arbitrarily determined (according to the number assigned to the deal), and are identical at each table at which the hand is played.

Since partials no longer count toward games, and games do not add up to rubbers, a numerical value is given to them. Whenever a contract is fulfilled, declarer's side scores an extra bonus:

50 for any partial
300 for a game, nonvulnerable
500 for a game, vulnerable

All other scoring (with one exception: honors do not count at most forms of duplicate) is the same as at rubber bridge. Trick score, slam bonuses, penalties, doubled overtricks, etc.—all are unchanged. Of course, there is no longer any distinction between **above** and **below** the line; in place of below-the-line scoring, declarer adds in the special bonus for making his contract. The score on any deal is expressed as a single number.

For example, suppose that your partnership holds the North-South cards on a hypothetical Deal 17; neither side is vulnerable. You bid three spades and make four. The score is +170: 120 for the four-odd tricks in a major suit added to the 50 bonus for fulfilling an undergame contract. (The plus sign indicates that the score was made by North-South; had the same score been made by East-West, it would be written "−170.")

Now, Deal 17 will be played at many other tables, and there are likely to be different results. Say that a North-South pair bids three spades, as you did, but wins only nine tricks. They score +140 (90 for the tricks, 50 for the partial). Another may bid *two* spades and make four. They score +170, the same result as yours. A third may bid a bold *four* spades and win ten tricks. This is +420 (120 for trick score, 300 bonus for a nonvulnerable game). A fourth North-South partnership might bid four spades and go down one. This is scored −50 (minus, since East-West scored the points). At a fifth table, East-West may sacrifice at five diamonds and go down two, doubled. The score is +300 (plus, since scores are written from the North-South viewpoint).

When the game is over, all these results (+420, +300, +170, +170, +140, −50) are compared. How did you do for +170? You beat two results, but were beaten by two and tied one. As we will see shortly, when we get to "match pointing" (see p. 8), your score is exactly average.

SCORING QUIZ

You and your partner are North-South. My partner and I are also North-South, playing the same cards, but at a different table, of course. Here are our different results on Deals 1, 2, 3 and 4.

DEAL 1
(neither side vulnerable)

700¹ + 240

+ 920   120
         300
         500

YOUR TABLE
Your opponents (East-West) bid three spades. You double and set them four tricks.

MY TABLE
We (North-South) bid and make six diamonds.

DEAL 2
(only N-S is vulnerable)

+ 670

+ 660   160
         500

YOUR TABLE
You are doubled in three clubs, and make your contract.

MY TABLE
We bid three notrump, and make five.

DEAL 3
(only E-W vulnerable)

← 620

— 280

YOUR TABLE
Your opponents bid four hearts and make it.

MY TABLE
We overbid to four spades, get doubled and go down three tricks.

DEAL 4
(both sides vulnerable)

+ 140 —   90
           50

YOUR TABLE
You bid two hearts, and make three.

MY TABLE
Our opponents bid three spades, we double and set them one trick.

On these four separate deals, what is the score at each table, and who did better, you or I?

Answers

DEAL 1. Your score is +700, the normal penalty for four tricks doubled, nonvulnerable. My score is +920 (120 for tricks, 300 bonus for nonvulnerable game, 500 bonus for nonvulnerable small slam). Obviously, I did better.

DEAL 2. Your score is +670 (120 is the double trick score, 500 bonus for vulnerable game—the bonus is not doubled—and 50 bonus for making a doubled contract). My score is +660 (160 in tricks, 500 for game). Your plus is larger, so you did better.

DEAL 3. Your score is −620 (120 for tricks and 500 for game). Mine is −500 (down three doubled, nonvulnerable). My minus is smaller, so my score is better. Note that on this vulnerability even a large set may cost less than an enemy game.

DEAL 4. Your score is +140 (90 for tricks, 50 for a partial). My score is +200 (down one doubled, vulnerable). So I win again (surely you didn't expect to beat me on my own quiz). Observe that 200 is a very special number at duplicate—it is larger than any normal part-score result.

THE MECHANICS

How is it arranged that one deal can be played many times? One of the techniques that makes this possible is a different (and, to rubber bridge enthusiasts, hard-to-get-used-to) manner of playing the cards themselves. Instead of casting cards into the center of the table to form tricks, duplicate players place their played cards face up in front of them. When all four cards to a trick have been played, each contestant (including the dummy, who handles his own cards at declarer's direction) turns his card face down *in front of him;* no one gathers in the trick.

In order to keep count of tricks won and lost, it is customary for each player to place a losing card, when he turns it over, parallel to the table's edge, "lying down"; a winning trick, in contrast, is indicated by placing the turned card at right angles to the edge, "standing up." Thus, in the illustration, you have lost the first two tricks, won the third and fourth, lost the fifth.

After all the tricks have been played and the result is agreed upon, each player picks up his original thirteen

cards—they are right on the table in front of him. He gathers them into a neat bundle, and places them face down into the appropriate pocket of the duplicate board.

The standard duplicate board is illustrated above. It is a shallow aluminum tray, marked with the number of the deal. There are four pockets, one of which is labeled "DEALER." Vulnerability is indicated also. On Board 19 above, "VUL" is lettered in red above the East and West pockets; in addition, the pockets themselves are red. The

North-South pockets are silver, and unmarked. Thus, East-West are vulnerable, North-South are nonvulnerable.

The geographical positions are marked, with a black arrow pointing to the North player. At the start of the game, the director in charge designates a direction as North, and the players take care to keep the arrow on each board pointing that way. (It is customary to leave the duplicate board in the center of the table even during play. This ensures that the hands will go back into their proper pockets.)

Let us see a typical duplicate game in operation. Suppose that fifty-two players, who have formed twenty-six partnerships or **pairs,** show up to compete. In a large room, there are thirteen card tables, numbered plainly from 1 to 13. The pairs fill up the tables, often being instructed by the director whether to sit North-South or East-West. Each partnership takes careful note of the table number at which it is to start play, for this determines its *pair number* for the whole game. For example, two partnerships start at Table 7: one is North-South Pair 7; the other East-West Pair 7.

Two duplicate boards containing cards are placed on each table. One player on each side removes all the cards from a board, shuffles his deck and deals it into four piles in front of him. Then he puts one pile in each pocket of the board. The first round is ready to start.

Each player picks his hand out of the pocket of the lower numbered board, and the bidding commences—starting with the player designated on the board as dealer. When play is completed and the result agreed to, each player puts his thirteen cards back in the pocket of the board. (It is best to count your cards, both before looking at them and before returning them to the board, to make sure the number is correct.) Now the North player must enter the result on the **traveling score slip** which accompanies each board (see illustration).

The example score indicates that on Board 13 (number in the top right-hand corner) North-South Pair 7 played against East-West Pair 7 (7 vs. 7 in the left column). East was declarer at four spades (4S/E in the column for final contract). Apparently declarer made eleven tricks, for the score is −650 (note that it is in the minus column; North scores his pluses on the left, his minuses on the right).

After North finishes scoring, East or West should check it for accuracy. The slip then is folded and placed in the

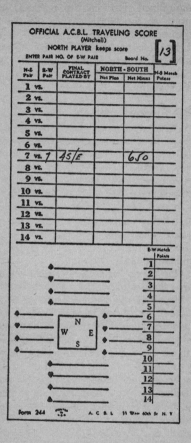

board. The second deal is then bid, played and scored. The whole process should take approximately fifteen minutes for the two-board round. Now, the director will call the change for the next round.

Each East-West pair moves to the next-higher-numbered table (from 6 to 7, from 10 to 11, from 13—the highest—to 1). The North-South pairs remain stationary, but move the boards just played to the next-lower-numbered table (from 4 to 3, from 1 to 13). And everyone settles down to bid, play and score new hands against new opponents. North writes the results on the traveling slips (obviously, no one looks at the traveling score until after play of the deal is complete), being careful to score opposite his own pair number, and to note the number of his new opponents. After fifteen minutes, a new change is called. Again, the East-West pairs move up and the boards move down.

After thirteen rounds, the game is over. Each pair will have played twenty-six deals; each deal will have been played thirteen times. (This game I have described has been run by the **Mitchell** movement, the most common type. However, there are other methods, usually for smaller numbers of pairs. In a **Howell** movement, almost all pairs move, not just East-West. At each table there is a **guide card** telling you where to go next. And, in either type of movement, different numbers of boards can be played, either in each round or in the whole game.)

MATCH POINTING

When the last round is over, the contestants can go home, but most (certainly, all who have played fairly well) will want to wait for the scores to be computed, to see who has won. Figuring the scores is a complicated job, and it is done by the directors who run the game; it is not necessary for any player to know how to do it. However, it is desirable to learn something about **match pointing**, for the scoring is basic to understanding the special features of duplicate.

Let us take another look at that traveling score slip for Board 13—the one we saw earlier. With the game over, it looks as illustrated.

Now all thirteen results can be seen, and, in the column at the far right, the director has filled in the match-point scores for each pair. Match points are computed as follows: A pair earns 1 point for each score that it beats (made by a pair holding the same cards); it earns ½ point for each score that it equals. North-South Pair 8, for example, beat every other North-South pair, to score 12 points (called a **top**). North-South Pair 10 was beaten by

OFFICIAL A.C.B.L. TRAVELING SCORE
(Mitchell)

NORTH PLAYER keeps score

ENTER PAIR NO. OF E.W PAIR　　Board No. [13]

N-S Pair	E-W Pair	FINAL CONTRACT PLAYED BY	NORTH - SOUTH		N-S Match Points
			Net Plus	Net Minus	
1 vs. 8		4S - E		650	3½
2 vs. 10		3NT /N		630	7
3 vs. 12		4S - E		620	9
4 vs. 1		4S/E		650	3½
5 vs. 3		3D - N X		200	11
6 vs. 5		4S/E		650	3½
7 vs. 7		4S/E		650	3½
8 vs. 9		6S - E	100		12
9 vs. 11		4S/E		620	9
10 vs. 13		5D/N X		800	0
11 vs. 2		4S/E		620	9
12 vs. 4		4S/E		650	3½
13 vs. 6		4S - E		650	3½
14 vs.					

	E-W Match Points
1	8½
2	3
3	1
4	8½
5	8½
6	8½
7	8½
8	8½
9	0
10	√
11	3
12	3
13	12
14	

Form 244　　A C B L　33 West 60th Sq. N. Y

all the other pairs and scored zero (a **bottom**). North-South Pair 2 beat seven pairs and tied none, for 7 points. North-South Pair 3 beat eight pairs (six who were −650, one −630 and one −800) and tied two pairs; to total 9 match points. North-South Pair 7 beat one pair and tied five pairs for 3½ points.

How are the East-West match points computed? It could be done the same way, but it is simpler to realize that 12 points are divided between the North-South and the East-West pair at each table. Thus, where North-South Pair 8 have a top, their opponents, East-West Pair 9, have a bottom. Where North-South earn 3½, their East-West opponents receive 8½; where North-South score 9, East-West score 3; and so on.

Several interesting conclusions can be drawn about the game of duplicate from the example score. One that shows up clearly is the importance of overtricks—witness the huge difference between the match-point score for —620 and that for —650. What counts at duplicate is simply how many results you beat, not how much you beat them by.

Something else you may notice—there can be a considerable element of luck in duplicate. Not, of course, in the cards *you* hold, but in what the opponents do with *their* cards. North-South Pair 10 no doubt richly deserved the bottom they scored for —800, but their opponents, East-West Pair 13, were presented with a lucky top. The same is true of North-South Pair 8, who were fortunate enough to have a bad slam bid against them. If enough opponents go berserk against you, you can play badly and still win; in contrast, if your opponents all play like geniuses, you will lose even though you and partner have your usual perfect session. However, these extremes are rare—the good and bad luck tend to average out, leaving your own efforts the determining factor.

Actually, your true opponents are not the ones who face you at the table. It is from the pairs at the other tables who hold your cards that you earn your match points. You must always think of these invisible opponents, trying to do as well as or better than they do on each deal. When the match-point scores of all the boards are added up, it is with these opponents—with the other pairs who sat in your direction—that you are compared.

When the totals are posted, the sheet will indicate what is "average"—50 percent of the possible match points. If your score is under average, you have been outplayed by your true opponents. If you are over average, you have done well. And if your score is somewhere between 60 and 65 percent of maximum, you may be the winner—the North-South or East-West pair who has done best of all.

TEAM CONTESTS

The type of duplicate game discussed so far is often called **match points**, or **match-pointed pairs**, or just plain **pairs.** Over 90 percent of duplicate competitions are pair games. The small balance are **team-of-four** contests, the form of competition generally considered the truest test of skill.

A **team** consists of two pairs (there may be as many as six members of a squad in major tournaments, but only four play at a time); one pair plays North-South, the other East-West at a different table. If Team A is pitted against Team B, a deal is played at Table 1 with the A pair North-South, the B pair East-West. Then it is re-played at Table 2 with the B pair North-South, the A pair East-West. Thus, if there is a possible slam with the North-South cards, each team has its chance to bid it. If a clever opening lead by East can defeat the contract, each team's East has his opportunity to be a hero.

A team match is an ideal form of duplicate for play at home. All you need is a set of duplicate boards, two bridge tables (preferably in different rooms) and eight bridge enthusiasts. Choose up sides, arrange the pairs properly in the two rooms, put Boards 1 through 4 at one table and Boards 5 through 8 at the other. Deal and play. After finishing the four boards, exchange boards with the other room, and play those deals. When you have played all eight boards, the first half is over and you can compare scores with your teammates.

Team A gathers in one room. The North-South pair adds its pluses * and minuses, and has a net score of −530. However, East-West has a net of +810. Team A has done better than Team B with the identical cards; it has won 280 points. Now, you can exchange opponents and play the second half—another eight boards—in the same fashion. A final comparison, and the winner of the match is determined. Almost always, it will be the team which has played better; virtually all luck factors have been eliminated.

* This is the one form of duplicate in which honors are scored.

This type of duplicate (called **total-point team-of-four**) is much the same as that used in deciding the World's Championship. Actually, a somewhat more complicated scoring system is used in important team tournaments. This will be described in Chapter VIII.

THE A.C.B.L.

The American Contract Bridge League *—the A.C.B.L. —is a nonprofit membership organization which supervises the duplicate activities of some two million players—in the United States, Canada, Mexico, various islands, and military and government posts all over the world. The A.C.B.L. has a huge variety of interests. It establishes the laws which regulate duplicate tournaments (and it helps write the rubber-bridge laws also); it publishes a monthly bridge magazine for its members; it has an ambitious charity program; it trains tournament directors; it promotes and publicizes duplicate bridge; through the World Bridge Federation, which it helped organize, it participates in international championships.

All this is in addition to the primary function of the A.C.B.L.—running duplicate tournaments of many different sorts. Most important are the three great national tournaments each year—Spring, Summer and Fall Nationals. Each of these is like a ten-day convention. They draw thousands of bridge enthusiasts from all over the country to play in clusters of widely varied contests—some major, some lesser, some minor. For example, a typical national tournament will contain one major championship for teams and one for pairs, each of which will attract almost all the leading stars, for victory may lead to a place on the American International Team. Each event will be played over six or eight sessions; either is likely to be open only to players of a certain rank. A National will also contain other championships—some restricted to men's or women's pairs, others to mixed pairs (a man playing with a woman) or mixed teams. Then, too, a National will include "consolation games" for those eliminated from major champion-

---

* For information, including a Directory of Affiliated Duplicate Bridge Clubs, write American Contract Bridge League, 33 West 60th Street, New York, N.Y. 10023.

ships and "side games" for those who do not wish to compete against the top players.

Next in importance are **regional** championships (the Eastern States Championship, for example). These may be held over a long weekend, or they may be ten-day "junior nationals." Again, they contain events of many sorts and of varying prestige. There are about thirty or forty of these regionals held throughout North America each year.

Sectional championships (for example, the Chicago championship) are much more common. There may be as many as fifteen or twenty of them around the country in one week. Typically, a sectional will be held over a weekend: Men's and Women's Pairs on Friday afternoon; Mixed Pairs Friday night; a two-session Open Pairs on Saturday; a two-session Team-of-Four game on Sunday.

Most duplicate, though, is played not in these formal tournaments but in clubs. Some six thousand clubs are affiliated with the A.C.B.L. and are franchised to run duplicate contests; usually these will be held once or twice a week, but some of the larger clubs have games every afternoon and every evening.

MASTER POINTS

In order to keep this vast tournament program in focus, and to keep a carrot dangling ahead of the nose of every duplicate enthusiast, the A.C.B.L. has a system of ranking all players—by **master points.** Each good showing in an A.C.B.L. event, whether it be a victory in the National Teams or a third place in a local club game, is rewarded with master points. Of course, the awards are roughly proportional to the importance of the contest. First place in a national might bring from 50 to 125 master points, depending on the class of the event; in a regional, 25 to 60 master points; in a sectional, 7 to 30 master points. In each case, there would be scaled-down awards for lower positions, and for minor triumphs like having the best score in the section, etc.

Victory in club duplicate games is rewarded with **rating points** (a rating point is one one-hundredth of a master point). For winning the Tuesday night duplicate in Peoria, you might receive 30 rating points. However, for each regular game, a club is entitled to hold, once a month, the

Monthly Master-Point game. Here, the award is a full master point (sometimes 2 points, in certain types of contests). And some clubs run **Club Championships** and **Winners' Games** which are entitled to higher awards.

The A.C.B.L. keeps accurate records of the accumulated master-point riches of each of its members. A player's first master point makes him a Junior Master; when he has 20 master points, he is a Master; 50 make a National Master; 100 make a Senior Master, 200 an Advanced Senior Master; and, finally, with 300 master points a player enters the highest stratum—he is a Life Master. (For the two highest ranks, a player must have won a specified number of **red points**—points won in regional or national competition.)

Of course, even Life Masters are greedy to add to their glittering hordes of master points, and, since master points accumulate over a lifetime, there are some fancy totals. I myself have about 6,000 master points, but this puts me only eighth on the list, far behind Oswald Jacoby who leads with 9,000 and Norman Kay who is second with 7,000. The truth is, I am sorry to say, that a player's master-point holding is not an exact measure of his ability—it is a far more accurate measure of the amount of time he spends playing bridge.

Still, master points count for a good deal. They are impressive—admit it, my 6,000 master points will get you to pay more attention to what I have to say. And you should see some "master" with 26 points lording it over his friends who have none!

RULES, PROPRIETIES AND ETHICS

Often the rubber-bridge player attending his first duplicate is shocked by the atmosphere of the game. He is likely to find his opponents cold, ruthless and rude. He comes to a table for a new round, sees a sweet young couple there, smiles warmly and says, "Good evening. How are you enjoying the game?" What reply does he get?

"Idiot! If you had returned the three of spades, we would have beaten that last hand two," the young husband snarls, to his wife, of course. He has not even heard the pleasantry addressed to him.

This is deplorable, to be sure, but it is understandable

as well. Duplicate is a contest, not a social occasion, and the players tend to get emotionally involved in their results, to become wound up in a competitive fervor. When our neophyte becomes a regular duplicate enthusiast, his bridge game will probably improve, but his table manners are almost certain to suffer. And his opponents will make allowances for him.

Another thing which is sure to disturb the beginning duplicate player is what happens when he commits some innocent infraction of the rules. Suppose he picks his cards out of the board and says "Pass"; but he is not the dealer. "*Director!*" bellows his right-hand opponent in stentorian tones. The director hurries to the table. "He passed out of turn," states the opponent, pointing an accusing finger at the culprit. Our newcomer shrinks in his chair, wondering if he will be thrown out of the club. But the director merely rules that he must pass at his first legal opportunity.

Somehow, it seems so harsh—like calling the police. But this is a necessary and routine part of duplicate bridge. Players are not allowed to settle such matters for themselves, as they would at rubber bridge; this is the director's job. And the rules must be strictly enforced. There must be no waiving of penalties. In a duplicate contest, other players' scores may be affected by what happens at your table, so there must be a different attitude toward infractions. In every case the director should be called to give the book ruling. Players soon realize that their opponents are not insulting them by calling for the director. It is all in the game.

The shadowy area of ethics and proprieties is another troublemaker for the newcomer. Ideally, no bridge player should ever give information to his partner by his mannerisms, tone or hesitations; no player who receives such illegal information should take advantage of it. Now, in the average home rubber bridge game, these proprieties are largely ignored. However, a more rigorous standard is expected in duplicate contests. If one partner goes into an anguished huddle and finally passes a 12-point hand, then the other partner opens the bidding light—well, nasty remarks may be made by the opponents.

Actually, one such situation is covered by the rules in duplicate. An unexpected preemptive opening bid or weak jump may cause an informative hesitation by an opponent. Therefore, before any such action, a player announces, "I am about to make a skip bid. Three spades." This skip-bid warning forces the next opponent to hesitate ten seconds before making any call. Thus, no inference can be drawn from his speed of action. This A.C.B.L. rule is a very good one, but, of course, causes a lot of grief to the beginner.

Still another source of annoyance is the abundance of new systems and conventions. Every partnership is expected to carry a private scorecard. Look at the inside of the card.

COMPARISON OF SCORES OR DISCUSSION OF HANDS WITH OTHER CONTESTANTS DURING A SESSION IS ILLEGAL AND SUBJECT TO PENALTY																	
Val.	Bd. No.	vs.	Contract & Declarer	Plus	Minus	Pts. Est.	Pts.	Bd. No.	Val.	Bd. No.	vs.	Contract & Declarer	Plus	Minus	Pts. Est.	Pts.	Bd. No.
None	1							33	None	17							49
N-S	2							34	N-S	18							50
E-W	3	7	3 N.T/E		630	0		35	E-W	19							51
Both	4							36	Both	20							52
N-S	5							37	N-S	21							53
E-W	6							38	E-W	22							54
Both	7							39	Both	23							55
None	8							40	None	24							56
E-W	9							41	E-W	25							57
Both	10							42	Both	26							58
None	11							43	None	27							59
N-S	12							44	N-S	28							60
Both	13							45	Both	29							61
None	14							46	None	30							62
N-S	15							47	N-S	31							63
E-W	16							48	E-W	32							64

American Contract Bridge League

PRIVATE SCORECARD—INSIDE

This side is strictly for your own convenience (and you must make sure that the opponents do not see it). Here you keep a record of your own game. The entry above indicates that you played Board 3 against Pair 7; that East was declarer at three notrump, and made ten tricks against you; that you consider this to be a disastrous result (undoubtedly, your partner made a serious error) and so have estimated a zero as your score. (It is a good idea to keep a running estimate. My own method is to go from 0 to 4: 0 for a ghastly result, 1 for a poor one, 2 for a normal score, 3 for a good result, and 4 for a bonanza.)

COMPETITIVE

Single Jump Overcalls:
Strong ☐: Intermediate ☐: Pre-emptive ☑
Over (weak) (strong) 1 NT ASTRO
Over weak 2's and 3's OPT. DBL
Unusual NT Overcalls (all levels) asks for:
Minors ☐: Unbid suits ☑
Direct 1 NT Overcalls: 15 to 18 H.C.P.
Overcall in opp's suit: { Majors MICHAELS
{ Minors MICHAELS

LEAD CONVENTIONS

MUD

CLASS 2 CONVENTIONS AND SYSTEMS

NEGATIVE + RESPONSIVE DOUBLES
WEAK JUMP SHIFT RESPONSES
STRONG SINGLE RAISE IN MAJOR
JACOBY TRANSFERS
FLINT
DRURY

OTHER BIDS, REBIDS, RESPONSES

PREEMPTIVE JUMP RAISE OF OVERCALL

OFFICIAL A.C.B.L. CONVENTION CARD

NAMES: T. Adams . P. Plumo   Pair Number 11

GENERAL APPROACH: Standard American ☐
Others: ROTH-STONE

Open 1 NT: 15 to 18 H.C.P.
Resp.: Stayman Forcing ☑
Gerber ☑ Other: __ Non-Forcing ☐
Weak 2 bids 6 to 12 H.C.P.
(Min. 6 - Max. 12)

Forcing Resp.
and Rebids { 2NT ONLY FORCE

Opening 2 Club forcing for:
Game ☑ 2 NT ☐ 3 of Major ☐

Do Not Open 4-Card Majors
1st/2nd Pos. ☑   3rd/4th Pos. ☑
1 NT Resp. to Major: Forcing 1 round ☐
1 NT Resp. to (1 ♣) (Minors) 9 to 11 H.C.P.
1 NT rebid by opener 13 to 15 H.C.P.
Psychics: Frequent ☑ Occasional ☐

Description
and Controls {

The outside of the card is for the convenience of the opponents. It lists all the agreements that you have with your partner. The opponents will study your announcements before starting play, and you should examine *their* card. It may look forbidding.

New duplicate players are sure to be frightened by a "loaded" announcement card like the one illustrated. They do not know what most of the cryptic notations mean; they do not understand why their opponents should use all these gadgets. Are they trying to take unfair advantage?

Quite the contrary. The opponents are being scrupulously fair, announcing—as they are legally bound to do—all their unusual understandings. The fact is that fancy bidding methods are rife in the world of duplicate. At rubber bridge, it pays to keep bidding simple, so as to get along adequately with many different partners. But in duplicate you find regular partnerships, playing together week after week. Here, newfangled systems and conventions to cover special situations can pay off handsomely. So, even if you do not want to use them yourself, you must study a lot of new devices.

The ones you must learn are covered in Chapter IX. It is a lot of work, I know, but it is not unnecessary bother. All the gadgets and gimmicks you must contend with are just one more element which help make duplicate the fascinating game it is.

II. MINORS, MAJORS OR NOTRUMP?

There are countless differences, some glaring and some subtle, between proper bidding at rubber and duplicate bridge. Virtually all of them can be traced directly to one peculiarity of duplicate scoring: what counts is how *many* scores you beat, not how *much* you beat them by.

The effect of this can be seen clearly in the bidding of these hands:

♠ J 10 6 5	♠ A K Q 8 4 2
♡ K 10 7 4 2	♡ A Q 3
◊ A J 8	◊ K 5
♣ A	♣ 7 2

PARTNER	YOU
1 ♡	2 ♠
3 ♠	4 NT
5 ♡	5 NT
6 ◊	7 NT

The auction above would be reproduced almost without variation at every single table in a typical duplicate game. In contrast, at rubber bridge the final bid would surely be seven spades.

Your seven-notrump bid would strike a rubber-bridge player as lunacy. What if the hearts split badly? Then the grand slam might go down in notrump while it is still lay-down in spades—a loss of 2300 points, an inconceivable disaster! At duplicate scoring, though, it would be just as disastrous to make seven spades (2210) when everyone else was making seven notrump (2220). You get as round a zero when all the scores beat yours by 10 points as you do when they beat yours by 2310.

Recently I saw two experienced rubber-bridge players, sitting down in a duplicate game for the first time, bid these hands:

♠ Q 4	♠ K J 7
♡ A K	♡ 8 4
◇ K 9 8 7 5	◇ A 6 4 2
♣ K 10 9 2	♣ A J 5 3

WEST	EAST
1 ◇	3 ◇
5 ◇	Pass

Trumps split evenly, and declarer guessed the two-way club finesse to make twelve tricks. West was pleased with his result, and was incredulous when I told him that he should have been in three notrump instead.

"Three notrump is a dangerous contract," he pointed out. "The opponents will lead hearts, and if diamonds do not divide two-two, they can force out my second heart stopper. Now I go down if I misguess in clubs. Five diamonds, though, is always cold. I win the heart lead and force out the ace of spades. If diamonds do not split, I cash my high spades and hearts, then endplay the opponents with their trump trick—there is no need to guess in clubs."

As you can see, West was a good bridge player, and he was absolutely right—but only at rubber bridge, where making the sure game is the important factor. At duplicate scoring, his result was atrocious. Every other East-West pair played in notrump, and even the one unfortunate declarer who made only ten tricks beat the score for five diamonds (430 to 420). I told East (who did not quite believe me) that I would have bid six diamonds over five on his auction. Mind you, I would expect to go down. But I refuse to submit tamely and accept my zero for playing five diamonds; rather, I would bid slam and seize some chance for a top score.

Now, do not get the idea that all contracts must be in notrump at duplicate. The basic structure of the game has not changed. Players who are so aware they are playing duplicate that they forget that they are playing bridge are invariably losers.

If you have tried duplicate, you know the players I mean. They will never, never play minor-suit contracts, and they won't play even in a major if they have the slightest excuse to bid notrump. Mind you, there is a germ of truth in their theories—tiny differences in trick score can yield bushels of match points. Sometimes. But when I play hands in a major suit, I usually beat the notrumpers by at least one trick; they make an extra 10 points, while I make an extra 30. And I get excellent results, as a rule, on the rare occasions when I elect to play in clubs or diamonds; I am not ashamed to score up my paltry little 20 per trick while the minor-haters are going down at some nobler contract.

Winning duplicate players are anxious to get to major-suit contracts, willing to play notrump, and mildly reluctant to end up in a minor suit. They know from experience that a suit contract will usually produce one to two more tricks than will a notrump contract. It works out that the most important consideration in deciding whether to try for a high-scoring declaration is whether you are headed for a part score, for a game or for a slam.

PART-SCORE BIDDING

It is in part-score bidding that you should strain least to play in notrump; that you should be most willing to play in minor suits. Let me illustrate this with a dull little hand taken from a recent duplicate game.

NORTH
- ♠ K J 7 4
- ♡ A Q 3
- ◇ 8 7 3
- ♣ 7 6 4

WEST
- ♠ 8 5 2
- ♡ K 8 4
- ◇ K J 9 6 5
- ♣ A 3

EAST
- ♠ A 9 3
- ♡ 10 9 7 6 5
- ◇ Q 2
- ♣ 9 8 2

SOUTH
- ♠ Q 10 6
- ♡ J 2
- ◇ A 10 4
- ♣ K Q J 10 5

South dealer. Neither side vulnerable.

At all tables, South opened one club; West usually over-called with one diamond; North bid one spade. And South had to pick a rebid: two clubs, two spades or one notrump. Which would you choose? Here were the actual North-South results in this 13-table game:

CONTRACT	N-S PLUS	N-S MINUS	MATCH POINTS
2 NT by South (made 4)	180		12
2 ♠ by South (made 2)	110		10½
2 ♣ by South (made 3)	110		10½
2 ♢ by West (down 2)	100		8
2 ♢ by West (down 2)	100		8
3 ♡ doubled by East (down 1)	100		8
1 NT by South (made 1)	90		4½
1 NT by South (made 1)	90		4½
1 NT by South (made 1)	90		4½
1 NT by South (made 1)	90		4½
2 NT by South (down 1)		50	1½
2 NT by South (down 1)		50	1½
2 ♡ by East (made 2)		110	0

Obviously, seven Souths rebid in notrump. One of them scored a top (probably against some fancy opening lead, like a heart), but most gained only fair or poor results. The suit contracts figured to and did win more tricks and more match points, even though they count less per trick.

Actually, if I were shown just the North-South cards, the contract I would pick would be in clubs. On the actual layout, North can make 140 at spades (notice, though, that the declarer who played there made only 110—a trick often disappears in "handling" these 4–3 trump suits), but if the enemy spades were divided 4–2, two spades might go down, for a terrible score. The club contract is certain to make, and did in fact score the same 110 as the riskier spade partial. (Do you see that low con-tracts in a minor can be attractive if they make one trick more than a major contract? Two clubs is better than one spade; three clubs is as good as two spades. Of course, this is not true for higher contracts.)

Observe the 6-match-point difference between the scores for +90 and +110. This is often the case, because on close competitive partial hands there figure to be quite a few scores of +100. In contrast, a score of +140 would earn only one point more than +110.

Notice, too, that no North-South pair which scored a plus was much under average—the terrible results were the minuses. This is true of most competitive part-score deals; you will not do very badly unless you are minus. In fact, one haphazard method of estimating your score after you have finished play is to add up your pluses and minuses: with a majority of pluses, you rate to be over average.

Thus, your first job is to play in the soundest partial contract, the spot most likely to produce a plus score. Your second job is to score 110 if you can. And as for your third job—getting the absolute maximum for a top—forget all about it. Let someone else gamble for the top; this wild man will take a bottom on the next hand and be back to average, while you are clipping along at a steady 65 percent pace for a winning score.

QUIZ I

The auction has gone:

YOU	OPPONENT	PARTNER	OPPONENT
1 ◇	Pass	1 NT	Pass
?			

What is your call with these hands?

(1) ♠ K 5   ♡ 10 2   ◇ K Q 10 8 2   ♣ A 8 6 4
(2) ♠ K Q   ♡ K 5   ◇ A K J 10 8 3   ♣ 10 8 2
(3) ♠ Q 8 4   ♡ A 7 3   ◇ A Q 8 4 2   ♣ 6 4

Answers

1. *Bid two clubs.* Your two doubletons make it highly probable that one, or more likely two, tricks extra can be won in a suit. Thus, even if partner could make two notrump for 120 (and this is remote), you may make four clubs or diamonds for 130. The minor-suit contract is your best bet both for a plus score and for 110.

2. *Bid three diamonds.* It is tempting to raise notrump, for if you have a game it is likely to be three notrump. However, partner will convert to three notrump if he has the few extra points you need. If he has not, and so will

pass your rebid, you want to be in the safe part-score contract of three diamonds not the dangerous one of two notrump.

3. *Pass.* Here you have uninteresting distribution and a poor suit. Therefore, one notrump figures to be safer than two diamonds. Note that it is not the extra points for notrump which induce you to pass—you choose the part-score contract most likely to yield a plus score.

GAME BIDDING

When your sights are set on a game contract, the whole picture changes. Merely getting a plus score is no longer your primary objective—the odds are that every single pair sitting your way will be plus when game can be made. So a low plus score can earn a zero; on game hands, you must try to score the biggest plus you can. Thus, you must almost never play *games* in clubs or diamonds.

Consider the strictly match-point bidding of these hands:

♠ 7 2	♠ A K Q 6
♡ A 8	♡ 7 4 3
◇ K Q J 9 4 2	◇ A 10 7 5
♣ Q 10 6	♣ 8 2

OPENER	RESPONDER
1 ◇	1 ♠
2 ◇ [1]	3 ◇ [2]
3 NT [3]	Pass

1. Note that opener rebids two diamonds, not one notrump. If responder is weak, opener should want to play a part score in diamonds, not notrump. (Suppose responder did not have the diamond ace, and so would pass opener's rebid. Then, one notrump would probably go down—possibly a lot—or at most make 90, while in diamonds a sure 110 and possible 130 is available.)

2. At rubber bridge, responder should probably jump to four diamonds here. But at match points, he must not risk going beyond the likely maximum contract. Hence, he underbids slightly to maintain his chance to reach three notrump.

3. When only a part score was in question, opener tried for the surest plus score in diamonds; now that game is in view, he tries for the largest plus score in notrump. Eleven tricks are sure at diamonds, but they score less than the likely ten tricks at notrump. The notrump game is not at all sure, for one time in ten a club lead will defeat it. Nine times out of ten, though, you will take a zero for playing in the safer five-diamond contract. Everyone else will make 30 points more at notrump—430 to 400.

Be sure to remember that the extra points are available in notrump only compared to a *minor*-suit game. A game played in a suit, when you have a good heart or spade fit, will usually produce at least 20 points more than will a notrump contract. Reverse the hearts and diamonds in the previous example and three notrump still is likely to make four (430); however, the suit game is sure for five, which is 450 in a major.

When you and partner have a 4–4 major-suit fit, you may feel an urge to try three notrump instead of the suit game. Resist that temptation—these are the deals which most often produce extra tricks in a trump contract. An inexperienced pair bid these hands against me:

♠ J 7 4 2	♠ A 8 6 3
♡ A 9 5	♡ K 4
◇ A 6	◇ K Q 7 5
♣ A J 9 4	♣ Q 10 2

OPENER	RESPONDER
1 ♣	1 ♠
2 ♠	3 NT
Pass	

They were delighted to make four (the club finesse worked), but could not have been pleased when they saw their match-point result. All the pairs who played spades made 11 tricks with ease. My opponents no doubt thought they were playing a clever duplicate style. But it is at rubber bridge that you should play these hands at three notrump: this game contract is the surest plus score since it can survive a bad spade split and a losing finesse. But four spades is the best bet for the largest plus and so is the correct contract at match points.

QUIZ 2

Partner opens with one notrump (16 to 18 points). What is your response with these hands?

(1)   ♠ K 6 4 2   ♡ A 7 3   ◇ 10 8 6 5   ♣ K 4
(2)   ♠ A Q J 9 8 3   ♡ 8 2   ◇ 6 5 3   ♣ 7 4
(3)   ♠ K 7 3   ♡ 9 7 2   ◇ A Q 9 7 6 4   ♣ 5

Answers

1. *Bid two clubs, Stayman.* Three notrump is very likely to make (and may be the safest game contract) but four spades will probably score an extra trick (if partner has a spade suit, and trumps break normally). So you must check for the 4–4 fit in a major before plunging into notrump.

2. Here, I would violate my principles and jump to *three notrump*. Note that it is not when I have a *four*-card major, but only when I have a long running suit, that I think about playing game in notrump instead of in the major; then there are no extra ruffing tricks available. The bareness of my hand suggests that we had better play for nine tricks instead of ten. (With a queen or two on the side, I would likely play in spades—the trump suit would give me time to set up secondary tricks which might be unavailable at notrump.)

3. *Bid three notrump.* There is no real choice. You cannot afford to play in five diamonds, since three notrump will score 430 or 460 most of the time. At rubber bridge I would worry about my singleton club; playing duplicate, I simply bid my three notrump and let my partner worry about the singleton.

SLAM BIDDING

You must vary your approach once more when it comes to slam hands. The policy of playing game contracts in the declaration that can produce the maximum result is based on this assumption (usually quite valid): virtually all the other pairs will be in game, too, when your side holds a combined count of 26 points or more. In contrast, this assumption does not hold true for slams on the skimpy side of the range—that is, slams bid on a combined count of 33 points or less. Here, most of the field will be only in game. Any slam that you bid and make will earn a magnificent score. So pick the safest contract. Suppose you hold:

♠ 5 3   ♡ K 4   ◇ K Q 9 8 3 2   ♣ A 7 4

Partner opens one notrump, you respond three diamonds, and partner raises to four diamonds. At this stage, you start regretting your somewhat ambitious response; perhaps you should have bid three notrump instead. However, you are now committed. That is, you cannot afford to play game in diamonds and you are already beyond three notrump. So you must go to slam—but in notrump or diamonds? Bid slam in the suit, since it is a doubtful contract. If the deal is:

♠ K Q 8	♠ 5 3
♡ A 10 3 2	♡ K 4
◇ A J 6 4	◇ K Q 9 8 3 2
♣ K 5	♣ A 7 4

you are cold for twelve tricks in diamonds. True, someone may bid six notrump and beat your score if the spade ace is on side. But you will get about 11 or 12 match points anyway just for +920. It hardly makes sense to risk a zero trying for 990, when it will earn only half a match point more.

However, I have been talking so far about touch-and-go slams which the field will not bid. When your side is so choked with high cards that your grandmother would bid slam, then you must get back to the idea of playing for maximum. For example, if partner opens one spade and you hold:

♠ A J 9 7 6 4   ♡ K J   ◇ K Q 7 2   ♣ A

Obviously, you will bid a small slam at least, but so will everyone else. Suppose you bid four notrump, Blackwood, and partner replies five diamonds. Bid six notrump. You are missing an ace, so this is unlikely to be a hand which will produce an extra trick in a suit. Go for the best possible score. Once in a blue moon, a club lead will defeat this contract, with six spades cold. Most of the time, though, you will have twelve tricks at either declaration, and the notrump bidders will get the good match-point scores.

As you see, a duplicate player with a notrump complex will have an occasional triumph. But if you play most of your hands at notrump you will be right only when you have a rock-crusher like the one above. And if you hold monstrous cards like these often enough, you are wasting your time playing duplicate. Go back to rubber bridge, and I will take half your game.

QUIZ 3

On this auction:

PARTNER	YOU
1 ◇	1 ♡
3 ◇	3 ♡
4 ♡	4 NT
5 ♡	?

Which slam would you bid with these hands?

(1) ♠ K 8   ♡ A K J 9 6 4   ◇ 7 3   ♣ Q 6 2

(2) ♠ K 5   ♡ K Q J 10 7 2   ◇ Q 6   ♣ A J 4

(3) ♠ 6 4   ♡ A K 7 5 4 3   ◇ K 8 5 2   ♣ A

Answers

1. *Bid six hearts*. It would be too greedy to bid six notrump, since many players will not bid slam at all. The heart contract figures to be safer, for you may have to ruff diamonds to set up partner's suit.

2. *Bid six notrump*. Now everyone else will be in slam, so you must try for the extra 10 points which are likely in notrump. The slight risk (that partner has a singleton club, and is missing a red ace) is well worth taking, for many match points are at stake.

3. *Bid seven diamonds*. Most of the other pairs will be in only a small slam (so if you settle for six, you will bid

hearts or notrump). Thus, when you decide to bid a grand slam, bid the safest one. Even if partner holds the heart queen it may be necessary to ruff one heart to set up the suit. Of course, some brave soul will bid seven notrump and make it for a top—if hearts behave. But for seven diamonds you will get 10 or 11 match points out of 12 without risking a zero—and 10's are good enough. The heroes who try desperately to snatch the cold top will usually be found where they belong by the end of the game—on the bottom.

III. THIRD- AND FOURTH-SEAT OPENING BIDS

Most experienced match-point players are likely to make feather-light opening bids opposite a passed partner. This style is much more advantageous at duplicate scoring than in rubber bridge, because the odds are different. You see, the rare loss caused by a skinny opening bid will be a heavy one—you may go for a big set, or partner may double an enemy contract that cannot be beaten. Those are disasters at any scoring, but at match points you can more than make up for an occasional catastrophe of this sort by a succession of small gains. At duplicate, what counts is not how much but how often you gain or lose.

THIRD-SEAT OPENINGS

Light third-hand openings can help in several different ways. First, they will pick up tricks for you on defense by directing a winning opening lead. Second, they have a nuisance value, using up the opponents' bidding room and making it harder for them to bid accurately. Third, they put your side in a superior competitive position—it is much safer to enter the auction with opening bids and raises than with subsequent overcalls. All these factors are apparent in the deal shown.

The defense started by cashing two spades, and later collected two club tricks—East-West scored 140. On the surface, this was no triumph for the light opening, but let us see how it affected the result.

First, North-South were able to compete up to two spades without great risk. (They would go down 300, but West can hardly double on this auction; he *could* double, though, if East opens, he raises and the opponents back in.) Second, South got off to a safe lead—left to his own devices he might well lead a club or diamond, allowing declarer to make four. Finally, East had a blind guess whether to to go on to game over three hearts. (West could easily

```
                    NORTH
                    ♠ K Q J 8
                    ♡ 5 4
                    ◇ 8 7 5 3
                    ♣ A 4 3

    WEST                         EAST
    ♠ 10 7 6 3                   ♠ 5 4
    ♡ Q 9 3                      ♡ A K 10 8 7 2
    ◇ K 6 2                      ◇ A J
    ♣ K 10 7                     ♣ J 6 5

                    SOUTH
                    ♠ A 9 2
                    ♡ J 6
                    ◇ Q 10 9 4
                    ♣ Q 9 8 2
```

SOUTH	WEST	NORTH	EAST
Pass	Pass	1 ♠	2 ♡
2 ♠	3 ♡	All pass	

hold K Q in clubs, for example.) Here East guessed right, but North-South will still be handsomely over average because of the lead; had he guessed wrong, North-South would score a near top.

If the light opening has such advantages, why not employ it in first and second position as well? Because then it will interfere with all the rest of your offensive auctions —you will never know when to bid game or slam. You cannot rebid intelligently when your opening bid can be anywhere from 10 to 22 points. The only reason that you can get away with outrageous openings after partner has passed is that you can now pass any response he makes. In this one factor, that opener can pass any response, lies the entire strategy of third- and fourth-hand openings, so keep it in mind at all times.

One way in which this affects your openings is in your choice of suit. Consider this hand:

♠ A K 10 2   ♡ 8 4 3   ◇ K Q   ♣ J 8 5 2

You should always be tempted to open one spade, as this is the suit you want led, and this bid has great preemptive value. But in first or second position, you must open one club, for if you open one spade, you have no sensible rebid over partner's change of suit. In contrast, you can and should open one spade after partner has passed. Your side cannot have enough for game, so you will pass a response of two hearts or two diamonds; there is no need to prepare a rebid. Likewise, this typical "short-club" opening bid:

♠ 843   ♡ A J 10 5   ◇ Q 6 4   ♣ A Q 2

is better opened one heart after partner has passed. There is no longer any need to distort your bidding to provide a rebid. Note, though, that you must still open one club with a hand like this one:

♠ A K J 5   ♡ A Q   ◇ 10 5 3   ♣ J 8 6 5

Here there is a reasonable chance for game even though partner has failed to open, so you cannot pass his response. Thus, you must plan your rebid. (If the heart queen were the deuce, I would open one spade. Now I must think about preemption and lead direction, not about my own game prospects. Now I can pass any response happily.)

The fact that you can pass partner's takeout allows you to open some of the example hands above in the suit you want led. It will also allow you to open hands that are considerably weaker. For instance:

(1)   ♠ A Q 10 6 4   ♡ J 5   ◇ K 3   ♣ 10 6 5 2
(2)   ♠ 9 6 2   ♡ K Q 10 3   ◇ A 8 7 3   ♣ J 2
(3)   ♠ 8 5 3   ♡ 10 6 2   ◇ A K Q 7   ♣ 6 5 4

In third seat, open (1) with one spade, (2) with one heart, (3) with one diamond. Remember, though, that you are opening despite your 9 or 10 or 11 points, not because of them. That is, your reason for opening is not to show your modest strength, but to direct a lead and to interfere with the enemy. Your safety comes not from some

mystic quality pertaining to third seat, but from the fact
that you can pass any response, staying low and warning
partner that your opening may be shaded. All three hands
above are good gambling third-seat openings because you
can bid the suit you want led and because you are prepared to pass any response. If either of these features is
missing, do *not* open.

(4) ♠ A J 8 4 2 ♡ 3 ◇ K J 4 ♣ J 10 6 3
(5) ♠ 8 6 ♡ K Q 6 ◇ J 9 7 4 3 ♣ K J 2

Pass both hands above. It is too dangerous to open (4),
since your partner is likely to respond with two hearts.
Now, you are in a fix—you do not want to pass, but you
confirm a sound opening (and will surely get too high) if
you bid. Hand (5) is safe enough to open, since you can
pass any response. However, there is nothing to gain by
opening one diamond; this bid will have little effect on the
opponents, and diamonds is not the suit you want partner
to lead.

You can see, in (4) above, that unbalanced hands are
unsuitable for light third-hand openings, since either a
long suit of your own or a side singleton will make you
unwilling to pass partner's response. One possible solution
is to open with a *three*-bid instead of a one-bid when your
suit is good enough. For example, with:

♠ 6 5 ♡ A K J 10 7 4 ◇ Q 8 4 2 ♣ 7

open three hearts after partner has passed. Some despera-
does of my acquaintance open with three-bids on weak
six-card suits or even on strong *five*-card suits after partner
has passed. However, you will have a superior alternative
here if you use weak two-bids in third or fourth seat. Then
you will have a complete range of satisfactory opening
bids: (1) a one-bid followed by your normal rebid, when
you hold a sound opening; (2) a one-bid followed by a
pass, when you hold a *balanced* 10 to 13 points and wish
to direct a lead or to impede the opponents; (3) a two-bid
when you hold 12 points or fewer, including a strong five-
card or weak six-card suit; (4) a three-bid, when you hold
an even better suit, but no game prospects.

QUIZ 4

What would be your action with these hands after two passes? What would you do as dealer?

(1) ♠ A Q 10 3   ♡ K 7   ◇ J 5   ♣ Q 8 6 5 2
(2) ♠ A K   ♡ 7 3   ◇ 8 4   ♣ K J 10 8 7 4 3
(3) ♠ A Q J 6   ♡ 10 8 5   ◇ K 7 5   ♣ Q 6 3
(4) ♠ 7   ♡ A Q J 8 5   ◇ Q 10 6 3   ♣ J 8 2
(5) ♠ A K 4   ♡ J 8 2   ◇ Q 7 5   ♣ J 7 5 4

Answers

1. *Open one spade in third seat.* You want a spade lead, and want the preemptive effect of the higher opening; you can pass any response. As dealer, *open one club* to provide a rebid.

2. *Open three clubs in third seat*—there is little chance for game once partner has passed, so try to buy the contract. As dealer, *open one club*.

3. *Open one spade in third seat.* This is the ideal light opening, for you are happy to pass any response. As dealer, you should *pass* or, in a sporting mood, open one club.

4. *Open two hearts in third seat* if playing weak two-bids. Otherwise pass. A one-bid is too dangerous in any position since you cannot pass a one-spade response.

5. *Pass* either as dealer or in third seat. If you feel like opening this hand one club, you have missed my point. A light opening is intended to direct a lead and to interfere with the opponents—one club does neither. If, however, you feel like opening one spade, you are on the right track. I probably would not enjoy playing *with* you, but I might not have a good time playing against you either.

OPENING IN FOURTH SEAT

Obviously, an opening bid in fourth position, after three passes, has an objective different from that of the typical light *third*-hand bid. You are no longer trying to impede the opponents or to direct an opening lead—you are after a plus score.

In deciding whether or not to open a substandard hand

in fourth position, you must keep three important factors in mind. (1) It is tempting to open since your side will theoretically be able to score a plus more often than not, once your right-hand opponent has failed to muster up a third-hand opening. However, (2) you will seldom be much under average for passing out a deal—this is true even when your side "owns" the hand for a small part score, since half the players who *do* open your hand will get too high. (3) The deciding factor is your holding in the major suits, with particular reference to spades, because it is the side with the higher-ranking suit which will usually score the plus when neither partnership has a decided advantage in point count.

Let me illustrate this with an example:

NORTH

♠ 9 2
♡ J 8 5 2
◊ A K 7 4
♣ Q 10 6

WEST

♠ K Q 10 8 3
♡ A 10 3
◊ J 5
♣ 5 4 2

EAST

♠ J 7 6 4
♡ K 9 7
◊ 8 3 2
♣ A 9 8

SOUTH

♠ A 5
♡ Q 6 4
◊ Q 10 9 6
♣ K J 7 3

The auction:

WEST	NORTH	EAST	SOUTH
Pass	Pass	Pass	1 ◊
1 ♠	2 ◊	2 ♠	Pass
Pass	3 ◊	All pass	

The contract was down one—South did not get the plus score that he opened for. Yet his side had more points than the enemy. In theory, North-South owned the hand, since they could make two diamonds while two spades could be defeated.

Who was at fault? Not North, certainly; his first response was conservative and he could not be expected to pass two spades. The answer is that South should not have opened the bidding. He could legitimately assume that his side would be in poor competitive position with its low-ranking suits. It seldom pays to open light in fourth seat with length in the minors.

In contrast, it does pay to open when you have spades. Suppose that *North* is the dealer in the preceding example, and there are three passes around to *West*. Should West open? Yes—he will probably get a plus score even though his partner has the poorest hand. The auction would likely start:

NORTH	EAST	SOUTH	WEST
Pass	Pass	Pass	1 ♠
Double	2 ♠	?	

South is certain to take action, and East-West will have a profit. It is the side which can push its opponents to the three-level which earns the plus—and this is the side which owns the high-ranking suit.

Once you have decided *whether* to open in fourth seat, the question of *what* to open is resolved in much the same fashion as in third position. There is no need to prepare a rebid, since you can pass partner's response. However, it is unwise to open in a ragged four-card major suit, for partner may raise (or even jump-raise) with three-card support. That is, suppose you hold one of these hands:

(1) ♠ K J 10 5 ♡ A 4 ◇ K 3 2 ♣ 10 7 5 3
(2) ♠ J 8 5 3 ♡ Q 6 4 3 ◇ A 7 ♣ A J 10

You should open in fourth seat, as you have the ranking suit. Bid one spade with (1), but bid one club with (2).

In fourth position, as well as in third, it is difficult to handle a hand like this one:

♠ K Q 10 9 4 ♡ 3 ◇ K J 8 4 ♣ J 5 2

If you open one spade, you cannot rebid sensibly over the likely two-heart response (if you rebid two spades, partner will expect a full opening and will get you overboard; if you pass two hearts, partner will not be pleased with the nature of your support). Yet this deal probably belongs to your side for two spades, so you hate to pass it out. The best solution, in my opinion, is to open with a weak two-spade bid. The weak two-bid is a very useful device for third- and fourth-hand openings. Particularly in fourth seat, it is wise to open with two on many hands which would qualify for a one-bid in first seat—for example:

♠ A K Q J 7 4   ♡ 10   ◇ Q 6 3   ♣ 8 7 3

If you were to open *one* spade, you might be pushed to three either by the opponents or by partner. Once partner has passed, there is little chance for game, so open *two*. The corollary is that if you do open *one* spade and then rebid your suit, you have game ambitions. (However, remember the A.C.B.L. rule limiting weak two-bids to 12 high-card points—if your singleton heart were the *jack* in the example above, you would be obliged to open one spade despite your meager game prospects.)

Opening three-bids in fourth position are game tries, not preempts. Three in a minor should promise a solid or near-solid suit with the high-card values for an opening one-bid; partner is expected to try three notrump with a smattering of stoppers. Three in a major promises seven or eight playing tricks; partner should raise to four if he can add two or three winners in aces, kings or ruffing tricks. These are typical fourth-hand three-bids:

♠ 7 4   ♡ K Q 10 9 8 6 3   ◇ A Q 5   ♣ 2
♠ J 6   ♡ A 3   ◇ A Q J 10 7 6 3   ♣ 7 5

Note that either hand would be opened with a one-bid in any other position.

QUIZ 5

What would be your action with the following hands in fourth seat after three passes? What would you do in third seat after two passes?

(1)	♠ 2	♡ 10 6 4	◇ A K Q 8 3	♣ Q 9 4 2
(2)	♠ A K J 5	♡ 8 3	◇ 10 6	♣ K J 10 7 4
(3)	♠ J 8 7 2	♡ A K 7	◇ Q 4	♣ J 9 8 3
(4)	♠ 7 5	♡ 8 6	◇ Q 7 4	♣ A K J 10 9 5

Answers

1. *Pass in fourth seat.* You probably have the best hand at the table, but you have nine cards in the minors and so do not figure to earn a plus score. *In third seat, open two diamonds* to interfere with the enemy auction and direct the opening lead.

2. *Open one club in fourth seat, one spade in third seat.* The difference is that you can assume, in fourth position, that *your* side owns the hand—you are trying to find out, as accurately as possible, what your best spot is. In contrast, when only one of your opponents has passed, *their* side may well own the hand. Thus, you should make use of the preemptive and lead-directing qualities of the one-spade opening.

3. *Open one club in fourth position.* You have better-than-average strength with seven cards in the majors, so your side figures to come out with a small plus score. However, *pass in third position.* Here there is no reason to suppose that you will buy the contract; and you certainly do not wish to suggest that partner lead clubs.

4. *Pass in fourth seat,* thanking your lucky stars that no one opened. (If your suit were spades, you would open —preferably with two.) A three-club opening is guaranteed to result in a minus, since if partner has enough to let you make three clubs, he will bid three notrump and go down there. However, *in third seat, open one club or three clubs,* depending on vulnerability. Now you are attempting to minimize your expected loss by telling partner what to lead and by using up the enemy bidding space.

RESPONDING AS A PASSED HAND

When partner has opened the bidding in third or fourth seat after you have passed, your problems as responder may be rather special. There are two complicating factors: (1) A change of suit is no longer forcing, so you must be prepared for a "sudden-death" pass of your response. (2) Partner may have opened a subminimum hand, to direct a lead or to try for a small plus score, and will then be annoyed if you get up too high.

Since any response you make may be passed, you must be very wary of responding in anemic suits. In general, the higher your response the greater is the chance that it will be dropped. This means that you can answer one diamond to one club with a weakish suit (four to the jack, say), since someone at the table will bail you out. But if you respond one heart, or more particularly, one spade, you should have a respectable four-card suit (at least four to the Q 10). And if your response is at the two-level, you must be prepared to play opposite a doubleton—partner is now as likely as not to pass. So you want to have a six-card suit or at least a husky five-carder.

Suppose that you have passed this hand:

♠ K Q 2   ♡ J 6 4 3   ◇ A 9 6 3 2   ♣ 7

If partner opens one *club*, respond one diamond. If, instead, he opens one *diamond*, respond three diamonds (not one heart as you might if it were forcing). If he opens one *heart*, you cannot temporize by answering two diamonds, so three hearts seems best. And if partner opens one *spade*, you must still avoid the two-diamond response, for you belong in spades not diamonds—you may choose between two and three spades, and the jump raise is probably better in the long run.

Likewise, if you have passed this hand:

♠ K 6   ♡ Q 10 4 2   ◇ K 10   ♣ K 9 6 3 2

you must be careful about bidding suits. Should partner open with one diamond, a one-heart response is preferable to two clubs. True, your *hand* is strong enough for a two-level response and for two bids; but (1) partner may pass before you get to make your second bid, (2) partner is more likely to find a rebid if he can do so at the one-level, and (3) if partner *does* pass, you would rather be in the higher-scoring major suit. What would you respond with this hand if partner opens one *spade?* Not two clubs, and certainly not two hearts, I hope. Your best bet is two no-trump; and this jump response could easily be right over one diamond or one club as well.

In contrast, if you have passed a hand that *does* contain a strong suit, you can give yourself a little more freedom in bidding it at the two-level. For example, holding:

♠ Q 7 5 2   ♡ 7 4   ◇ 2   ♣ K Q 10 8 6 3

I would respond two clubs to a one-diamond opening *if I were a passed hand,* while I would respond one spade if I were not. What makes the difference? Once I have passed, there is a fighting chance to play in two clubs when I bid it; and if partner rebids two diamonds, I can carry on with two spades without creating forcing situations. What is more, it is dangerous to respond one spade—if partner passes, there is no reason to believe that we are in either the safest or most productive contract.

Since the requirements for a two-over-one new-suit takeout are shaded down, you must worry about missing game when you have the normal solid values for this response. Consider these hands:

♠ 8 3   ♡ K Q 10 8 7 4 2   ◇ A 10 5   ♣ 5
♠ 7 4   ♡ 6 2   ◇ 8 5   ♣ A K Q 10 9 6 5

If, for some reason that appealed to you at the time, you have passed either hand, *jump-shift* over partner's opening. *Two* hearts or *two* clubs in response to one spade is no longer nearly enough; you must jump to three. This puts partner on notice that you have game ambitions even opposite the bare minimum opening bid with which partner would pass a simple response.

Does it worry you to jump so freely as a passed hand, when partner can have such sparse values for his opening? It should. The last two examples are safe enough at the three-level, for you have seven winners and partner should have the decency to provide two. But passed-hand jump raises and jumps to two notrump entail considerable risk of minus scores. Consider these hands:

♠ K 8 6 2	♠ A Q J 9
♡ J 10 4	♡ 7 5 3
◇ A Q 7 5	◇ 10 2
♣ 7 3	♣ K 10 8 2

WEST	EAST
Pass	1 ♠
3 ♠	Pass

No one made a bad bid—East's third-hand opening is irreproachable, and West has the values for a passed-hand jump raise—but the final contract is dangerously high. Unless two finesses succeed, it will go down for a poor score. How do East-West get to *two* spades? It is no solution for West to temporize with two diamonds, as he might had partner opened in *first* seat, for he will be left in this unappetizing contract. Some players might bid only two spades with the West hand, fearing a light opening, but this risks missing game opposite a sound minimum. The range of the single raise becomes impossibly broad (unless these players bid in delicately graded intonations; then they will get into a different kind of trouble).

Here is a similar problem:

♠ J 8 7 3	♠ 9 6 2
♡ Q 10 4	♡ A K J 2
◇ K J	◇ Q 10 9 4
♣ A 9 4 2	♣ J 6

WEST	EAST
Pass	1 ♡
2 NT	Pass

This contract is not likely to be a success: what went wrong? Surely, West could not bid only *one* notrump or two hearts; *three* hearts is a possible response, but is almost certainly down one. A response of one spade would be passed, and declarer can develop ulcers playing in a trump suit like that. Perhaps light third- and fourth-hand openings are for the birds.

Not really. You will show a big match-point profit in

the long run by opening these hands. When partner has a
normal minimum count, you will earn a small plus or at
least impede the opponents or direct a good lead. The examples above are unlucky, but there is an answer for them
too.

My suggestion is that you adopt the Drury convention.
When the bidding is opened in third or fourth seat with
one of a major, the response of *two clubs*, by the passed
hand, is artificial. It asks opener, "Do you have a normal
bid, or have you opened light?" If opener has shaded his
values, he answers *two diamonds;* if he has a reasonable
hand, he makes his natural rebid and the auction proceeds
normally.

In the examples above, West would respond two clubs,
Drury. East would rebid two diamonds, and West would
sign off safely at two of opener's major. Let us see an auction where opener has his full bid:

♠ K 7 2	♠ A Q 10 8 4
♡ A Q J 3	♡ K 10 6 2
◇ Q 7 6 2	◇ 9 8
♣ 8 6	♣ A 5

WEST	EAST
Pass	1 ♠
2 ♣	2 ♡
4 ♡	Pass

Here, the advantage of Drury is in making it easy to find
the heart fit; without it, West would likely jump to three
spades. However, the principal use of this convention is
in staying at the two-level in case East's opening bid is:

♠ A J 9 8 4   ♡ 6 2   ◇ 9 8 4   ♣ A J 5

Then, the auction would go:

WEST	EAST
Pass	1 ♠
2 ♣	2 ◇
2 ♠	Pass

QUIZ 6

You pass these hands, and partner opens one heart in third seat. What is your response?

(1) ♠ 10963 ♥ Q7 ♦ AJ762 ♣ QJ
(2) ♠ 82 ♥ Q75 ♦ AJ10953 ♣ 76
(3) ♠ 106 ♥ K982 ♦ AQ8632 ♣ 7
(4) ♠ 62 ♥ AJ85 ♦ AJ96532 ♣ Void

Answers

1. *Respond one notrump.* Your hand is a trifle strong, but neither your spades nor your diamonds are husky enough to bid at the requisite level. You are closer to *one* notrump than to *two*. Drury is no help here, for you have nowhere to go if partner answers two diamonds.

2. *Respond two diamonds.* If partner has opened light, your best shot for a plus score is in diamonds, not in hearts, so do not be greedy and raise. Do not get cute and use Drury, intending to pass two diamonds; if partner bids anything else you can never describe your hand.

3. *Jump to four hearts*—three hearts is not enough, for you can make game opposite junk. If you use Drury, you might bid two clubs, intending to jump to game over a two-diamond reply and to try for slam if the reply is anything else.

4. Did you really swallow that original pass on these cards? If you pass hands like this, you deserve insoluble problems. Give up the game, or take up the Roth-Stone system.

IV. SACRIFICE BIDDING

Sacrifice bidding over enemy game contracts can be much more profitable at duplicate scoring than at rubber bridge. You will never see a successful "money" player chortling with triumph after going down 500 to stop a vulnerable game—he has saved very few points, if any, and would rather have had whatever small chance there was of setting the opponents' contract. However, losing 500 instead of 620 at duplicate can yield a huge match-point score.

THE ODDS

Remember, though, that you will earn a fat score with your sacrifice only when most of the field is bidding game with your opponents' cards. Suppose that you hold this hand, nonvulnerable against vulnerable:

♠ J85 ♡ 862 ◇ J7 ♣ K10764

The auction goes:

OPENER	YOU	RESPONDER	PARTNER
1 ♡	Pass	2 ♡	2 ♠
3 ♡	Pass	Pass	3 ♠
Pass	Pass	4 ♡	Pass
Pass	?		

Should you sacrifice? The enemy will make their game more often than not—you have too good a fit with partner and too little defense to expect a set. Certainly, you will go down 500 or less at four spades. But you should *pass*, for the odds do not favor a sacrifice. The auction makes it clear that most of the 12 other pairs who hold the opponents' cards will *not* be in game. Say that this deal is played in a part score eight times, in four hearts twice, in four spades doubled twice. Then, if four hearts makes, you will score 1 point for letting it play, or 3 points for saving; if four hearts goes down, you score 11 points for letting it play or 1 point for saving. So you stand to gain 2 or lose 10—and the odds are nowhere near 5 to 1 that the game will make.

In contrast, suppose that you hold the same hand on *this* auction:

OPENER	YOU	RESPONDER	PARTNER
1 ♡	Pass	3 ♡	3 ♠
4 ♡	?		

Now, the whole field is likely to be in game. Say that six pairs are allowed to play four hearts while the other six double four spades. Either for passing or for bidding four spades you will score 9 points if you are right, 3 points if you are wrong—it is an even money bet. At these odds, the price is right for a sacrifice, since four hearts will make perhaps three-quarters of the time.

Thus, the most important factor in sacrifice bidding at duplicate is the sound of the enemy bidding: be reluctant to sacrifice when the opponents stagger into game even if you think they are likely to make; be alert to sacrifice against confident auctions, when it appears that everyone else will be in game too.

VULNERABILITY

Next in importance is the vulnerability. To be set more than the value of the enemy game is irritating at any scoring, but it is a major disaster at match points. Thus, you never really "sacrifice" when the vulnerability is **unfavorable** (you are, they aren't). If you outbid the opponents, it must be with some notion that your contract might make; then if you go down, you will be down only one. On **equal** vulnerability (both vulnerable or no one vulnerable), you can loosen up, outbidding the opponents even when you are certainly going down. Here, you should have some hope of going down only one; otherwise, there is too much danger of down three for a zero. You cannot be really frisky with your sacrifice bidding unless the vulnerability is **favorable** (the opponents are and you are not) so that you can afford down three. For instance, suppose you hold:

♠ 2   ♡ A Q J 8 4   ◇ 8 5 2   ♣ K Q 9 4

You open one heart; left-hand opponent doubles; partner raises to two hearts; and right-hand opponent jumps to four spades. It sounds as though the opponents have bid a normal game—should you sacrifice? Obviously, you will pass if the vulnerability is unfavorable; you have no chance to win ten or eleven tricks. Equally obviously, you will bid five hearts if vulnerability is favorable; the opponents are more likely than not to make their game, and have little prospect of beating you 700.

What about equal vulnerability? The single most probable result, I would guess, is that the opponents can make their game while you will be down only two. But I advise a *pass*. The combination of two less likely chances—(1) that you might beat four spades, plus (2) that you might go down three—outweighs the single most likely one. The opponents are merely favorites to make game—they could easily go down. And you are merely a favorite to win nine tricks—after a single raise, you would not have contemplated a try for game, and this means that you have no assurance of making *three* hearts.

A hidden advantage of sacrifice bidding is the chance that the opponents will be pushed one higher and will go down. This accentuates the vulnerability difference. On unfavorable vulnerability, the opponents are longing to double you; on equal vulnerability they are willing to double; but on favorable vulnerability, they are reluctant to double and may well be pushed overboard. When the vulnerability is favorable, the odds on sacrifice bidding are simply magnificent. You should consider sacrificing against a confidently bid game whenever you and partner have a suit fit plus a little distribution. I would estimate that there is a paying nonvulnerable sacrifice against a vulnerable suit game between one-third and one-half the time.

This means that you must charge into the auction very boldly when the vulnerability is favorable. Loosen up your takeout doubles, and forget about all the strict requirements for overcalls. Any time you have exciting distribution, get in there and bid. Do not worry about point count. The weaker your hand, the more likely the opponents are to have a vulnerable game. It is *safe* to bid, since the opponents hate to double low contracts when they may have to beat them 700; and it is *rewarding* to bid, for you will find most of your good saves. A hand like:

♠ 63   ♡ 4   ◇ K 10 7 3   ♣ Q 8 7 4 3 2

does not meet the requirements set for an overcall in any book I have ever read (or written), but I would surely bid with it—if partner has a club fit, we have a good sacrifice.

When partner has overcalled on this vulnerability, raise him whenever you have a fit. His assumption should always be that you are looking for a sacrifice, not for a game. But be wary of raising when you have a good deal of *defensive* strength. For example, suppose you hold:

♠ Q 10 4   ♡ Q J 8 6   ◇ 8 5   ♣ K Q 10 2

Your left-hand opponent opens one club, partner overcalls one spade, right-hand opponent bids two hearts. You should *pass*. On *unfavorable* vulnerability, raise to two spades; if partner bids four spades, he expects to make it, and he will. However, on favorable vulnerability he will bid four spades as a sacrifice, and probably the enemy have no game.

AGAINST SLAMS

If your opponents can make a vulnerable slam, a nonvulnerable sacrifice is almost certain to be cheap; their slam is worth at least 1370, while even down *seven* costs you only 1300. And if they have a vulnerable grand slam, a truly ridiculous situation exists: down *eleven* is a profitable sacrifice nonvulnerable.

Therefore, on this vulnerability you should climb into the auction with the slightest justification, the instant that the enemy bidding takes a slammish turn. (A strong two-bid faced by a positive response, a jump-shift response to an opening bid—these are the sort of sequences I mean.) Your competition may impede the opponents, particularly if partner is able to raise your suit, taking away their bidding room and causing them to bid less accurately. And if they reach the slam for which they seem headed, you will have found the suit in which to take a sacrifice that is virtually guaranteed to be cheap.

Unfortunately, however, there is *no* guarantee that your cheap sacrifice will earn you a good match-point score. If you save at seven diamonds over six spades and go down 1100 when the opponents would have made 1430, you will be rewarded with a high score only when most pairs are reaching slam with the opponents' cards; if the contract was an unusual one, your score will be disastrous even though your decision was "correct." And slams are likely to be unusual contracts. So, sacrifice only against the most confident, bouncy enemy auctions; if the opponents have stretched to reach slam, tend to let them play. This applies even more strongly to *grand* slams, which are always unusual contracts: a sacrifice against a grand slam will almost never score over average, so the slightest chance for a set (which will yield a top) should be preferred.

QUIZ 7

You are South, holding:

♠ Q 8 4   ♡ 3   ◇ K J 8 6 5   ♣ 8 4 3 2

What is your call on these auctions?

1. You are vulnerable; they are not.

WEST	NORTH	EAST	SOUTH
1 ♡	Double	Redouble	Pass
2 ♣	2 ♠	4 ♡	?

2. They are vulnerable; you are not.

WEST	NORTH	EAST	SOUTH
1 ♡	2 ♣	3 ♡	?

3. They are vulnerable; you are not.

WEST	NORTH	EAST	SOUTH
1 ♡	1 ♠	2 ◇	?

4. They are vulnerable; you are not.

WEST	NORTH	EAST	SOUTH
Pass	1 ◇	Pass	2 ◇
Double	3 ◇	3 ♡	Pass
4 ♡	Pass	Pass	?

5. They are vulnerable; you are not.

WEST	NORTH	EAST	SOUTH
1 ♡	1 ♠	3 ♣	3 ♠
5 ♣	Pass	6 ♣	?

Answers

1. *Bid four spades.* You would have tried for game even if East had passed partner's two-spade bid. Thus, you are not really "saving"; maybe you can make game. And maybe *they* can make game and you are down one. And maybe they will save against *your* game contract.

2. *Bid five clubs.* The opponents are on their way to a normal game contract, and you intend to sacrifice. Do so right away.

3. *Bid two spades.* Here, you have no intention of sacrificing if the opponents bid game. However, you should show partner your support so that *he* can sacrifice if he has very little defensive strength.

4. *Pass,* despite your feeling that a five-diamond sacrifice will be a good one—that is, that four hearts is likely to make while you will go down only 300 or 500. The trouble is that too few East-West pairs will reach game. Remember, West passed originally, and East could not act over one diamond. Thus, you are settling for a poor score if you save. Your only chance for a good score is to pass and pray.

5. *Bid six spades.* You cannot be set too much on this

vulnerability. The slam figures to make, since your high cards are in "'your" suits not theirs. And, most important, their auction sounds so strong that you can expect almost all the other East-West pairs to bid slam.

WHO SHOULD SACRIFICE?

So far, we have explored the odds on sacrifice bidding at duplicate, concluding that the price is right only when the opponents have bid confidently (so that most of the field is in game) and when the vulnerability is favorable (so that down three is a good result instead of a zero). When the opponents are vulnerable and you are not, it pays to enter the auction very light in order to set up a possible save.

However, once you and partner start bidding freely on a king and a prayer, you have to guard against the danger of taking "phantom" sacrifices against nonexistent games. After all, vigorous competition may have forced the opponents to overbid. And a shrewd opponent may bounce confidently into game on a contested auction when what he is sure of is not that he can make his contract but that you will save against it. You overcall and raise loosely so that your side is in a position to sacrifice if it wishes to. But you must not always wish to.

The answer is to refuse to save when you have fair defensive strength; the member of the partnership who decides to sacrifice must be the one who is weak defensively. This way, your side will never sacrifice when each of you holds a couple of defensive tricks, so that between you you have enough to set the enemy game. Suppose you hold one of these hands, nonvulnerable against vulnerable opponents:

(1) ♠ 87 ♥ K5 ♦ A 10 8 7 6 2 ♣ Q 5 4
(2) ♠ 8 7 5 ♥ A 9 2 ♦ J 10 8 7 6 2 ♣ 4

The auction goes:

OPPONENT	YOU	RESPONDER	PARTNER
1 ♣	1 ♦	1 ♠	2 ♦
4 ♠	?		

Should you bid five diamonds? Not with hand (1)—your defensive chances are too good. You will probably win two or three tricks yourself and partner figures to contribute something. It sounds as though opener may be stabbing wildly, trying to stampede you into a sacrifice. In contrast, bid five diamonds with hand (2), for you have no prospect of two defensive tricks. Partner would not raise, encouraging you to save, if he could win three tricks on defense. Note that the key consideration (on favorable vulnerability) is whether you can defeat them; you assume, once you have found a fit and have some distributional assets, that you can hold the penalty to 500.

Now let us look at partner's role in the auction above. Obviously he has a fair to middling hand with diamond support, but this could mean either of these:

(3) ♠ 9 3 ♡ Q 10 8 4 ◇ K Q 4 ♣ K 8 6 2
(4) ♠ 3 ♡ 8 7 6 4 3 ◇ K Q 9 4 ♣ 10 8 2

If partner holds hand (3), he should raise diamonds and then leave all sacrifice bidding to you. However, if partner holds hand (4), it is *his* responsibility to take the save. He has reasonable offensive values, and his hand is worse than worthless for defense.

PREMATURE SACRIFICE

The fact is that if I raised my partner's one-diamond overcall to two diamonds, I would always have a hand like (3) above—a smattering of defensive cards, so that I do not intend to sacrifice, but support for partner so that I am willing to hear *him* save if he has very little defense. When I hold a hand like example (4), with which I intend to sacrifice all by myself eventually, I sacrifice *right away;* I would jump to five diamonds at my first turn. I have a weak hand with a good fit for partner, so the opponents have a fit also and enough cards to bid and make game. If I hide my head in the sand and hope that their game will disappear, saving only after they bid it, they will have exchanged enough information to enable them to make an accurate decision at the five-level. But if I sacrifice immediately, they will be guessing in the dark.

The whole deal might be:

NORTH
♠ Q 10 9 5 4 2
♡ J 10 9
◇ 3
♣ A 9 3

WEST
♠ 8 7
♡ K 5
◇ A 10 8 7 6 2
♣ Q 5 4

EAST
♠ 3
♡ 8 7 6 4 3
◇ K Q 9 4
♣ 10 8 2

SOUTH
♠ A K J 6
♡ A Q 2
◇ J 5
♣ K J 7 6

Notice that East-West have a good save at five diamonds, while North-South will probably make only ten
tricks at spades (there are two ways of making eleven
tricks double-dummy, but neither is a likely line of play).
So the pairs who allow four spades to play will do poorly;
those who save will be over average. The top will go to
the East-West pair that has this auction:

SOUTH	WEST	NORTH	EAST
1 ♣	1 ◇	1 ♠	5 ◇
5 ♠	Pass	Pass	Pass

The moral is to sacrifice as soon as possible, bidding
right away as high as you are willing to go later. This
gives you your best chance to push the opponents overboard.

AT THE FIVE-LEVEL

If your sacrifice *does* succeed in pushing the enemy to
five of a major, you and partner should almost always let
them play there. Do not double; do not sacrifice further.
In the previous example deal, East-West have a paying

sacrifice at *six* diamonds (they will go down only 500 while North-South might make 650 if allowed to play five spades); but it is wrong to bid six diamonds over five spades. North-South are likely to go down at five spades, but West would be foolhardy to double. The reason, in both cases, is that the odds are wrong.

You see, when you sacrifice at *six* diamonds, you are running a much greater risk of going down 700 for a cold zero. In return for this risk, you no longer stand a chance to earn a really good score—you will lose to all the pairs who buy the contract for *five* diamonds doubled. So you are betting a zero against the average by sacrificing over five spades; by allowing the opponents to play in five spades, you may earn a top, while at worst you will get a slightly below average score.

The odds are even more clearly against doubling five spades. Just for defeating this contract undoubled, you will earn almost all the points—the double is unlikely to gain as much as 1 full match point. However, the double will cost you 3 or 4 match points when it goes wrong, since otherwise you would have tied the pairs who defended against normal *four*-spade contracts.

When your sacrifice pushes your opponents to five, take your profit and pass. The old Wall Street adage applies here: sometimes the bulls win, and sometimes the bears win, but the pigs always lose.

QUIZ 8

You are West, nonvulnerable against vulnerable opponents, and your hand is:

♠ 8　♡ K J 10 8 3　◇ Q 7 5　♣ K 10 6 4

What action do you take on these auctions?

	SOUTH	WEST	NORTH	EAST
(1)	Pass	Pass	1 ♠	2 ◇
	3 ♠	?		
(2)	Pass	Pass	1 ♠	2 ♡
	3 ♠	?		

(3)   1 ♠   2 ♡   2 ♠   3 ♡
        4 ♠   ?

(4)   1 ♠   2 ♡   4 ♠   5 ♣
        5 ♠   ?

Answers

1. *Bid four diamonds.* You are perfectly willing to hear partner sacrifice if his values are distributional, but this is not the sort of hand with which to bid five diamonds all by yourself. If North bids four spades and partner passes, you will pass also. You are likely to win two tricks on defense, so if partner has hopes of defeating an enemy game, you have, too.

2. *Bid five hearts.* Contrast this with (1). Here you have much less defense, both because of your wasted honors in partner's suit and your great length there which detracts from *partner's* defensive prospects. Therefore, you intend to sacrifice over four spades. Do so immediately for maximum effectiveness.

3. *Pass.* Your honors in the minor suits could produce defensive tricks, and your chances for a heart trick are fair since you have only a five-card suit. Thus, you have too much defense to save. Remember, partner is likely to have a smattering of honors for his raise—if he were defenseless, he would have done more than bid three hearts.

4. *Pass.* It is tempting to save at six clubs, since you certainly should be down only 500 or less, but consider your prospects. If you let five spades play, you will have a top if North-South can make only ten tricks, or a fine score if they can make twelve tricks; and even when they make exactly eleven tricks, you will get a few points. When you get the chance for a top without the risk of a bottom, seize it. You will not win many master points settling for average.

V. TRAPPING AND BALANCING

The double of an enemy opening suit bid is for takeout —there is no way to make a penalty double. This means that you will hold many strong hands, long in the enemy suit but too weak or too unbalanced for a one-notrump overcall, for which there is no appropriate action. You must pass, lying low like a snake in the grass, hoping that the opponents will get overboard. You should **trap-pass** over a one-spade opening with:

(1)	♠ K J 9 6 4	♡ A 5	◇ K Q 8	♣ J 9 2
(2)	♠ Q J 9 8 6 2	♡ K J 7	◇ A K	♣ 6 4
(3)	♠ A Q 10 2	♡ A K 9 3	◇ Q J 8 2	♣ 7

If the auction should proceed:

OPENER	YOU	RESPONDER	PARTNER
1 ♠	Pass	1 NT	Pass
2 ♠ (or pass)	?		

you will then double for penalties, springing your trap. This sort of double is not cooperative; partner must leave it in almost regardless of his hand. You must not double without the high-card strength of the examples above, no matter how good your spades. After all, responder may run to another suit, and partner may double *that*.

REOPENING

The trap pass is made in the hope that responder will act over the opening bid and land in serious trouble, but half the time he will pass the opening. If your partner passes also, you may get a foul result—plus 50 or 100 when you could make a big part score or even a game. Therefore, if *you* are in the pass-out position, in fourth seat on an auction like:

OPENER	PARTNER	RESPONDER	YOU
1 ♡	Pass	Pass	?

try to **balance,** to keep the bidding alive. Suppose, on the auction above, you hold:

♠ 8 4 2   ♡ 6   ◇ K Q 10 9 4 2   ♣ 10 5 3

Bid two diamonds. Why act with only 5 high-card points after partner has passed? Because partner is marked with strength—he could easily have the best hand at the table. After all, there are 40 points in the deck. Give opener 16 and responder 4—more than either needs for his action. Still partner has 15 points. Clearly, he passed not because he was weak but because he was long in hearts; at the very least, he has a sound opening bid. And would you have let the enemy play in one heart if partner had opened?

This balancing overcall means that you are bidding *partner's* cards. He must not "rebid" these same values by leaping about—rather, he must be very cautious when you reopen with an overcall. The corollary is that if you have the strength for an independent bid of your own, you should usually balance with a takeout double. If a one-spade opening is passed around to you, reopen with a double holding any one of these hands:

(4)	♠ 7	♡ 8 4 3 2	◇ A Q 9	♣ A K 10 7 6
(5)	♠ A 2	♡ A 8 6 3	◇ 7 3 2	♣ Q 10 8 4
(6)	♠ 5 4	♡ A K Q 9 6	◇ 7 3	♣ K J 8 4

This has two advantages: (1) Partner will realize that you have substantial high-card strength. (2) Partner can pass for penalties if he was trapping. Beware of a reopening double with fewer than 10 high-card points—partner is likely to make a penalty pass, and neither one of you will be pleased with the result.

When you balance with a double, partner should make a minimum response even with a moderately strong hand. If you hold a normal, fairly powerful double like example (4), you will raise his response. Holding hand (6), with which you would overcall in the direct position, bid your suit over the response. You pass partner's reply only with a scratchy, strictly balancing double like example (5). Thus, partner need not take violent action unless he has a power-house.

There are a few awkward distributional patterns in the reopening seat. For example, suppose that a one-heart opening is passed around to you, and you hold:

♠ 7 5   ♡ 8 2   ◇ Q 7 4   ♣ A K Q J 8 6

A balancing overcall does not do justice to your strength, but a reopening double has two flaws—you do not want to hear partner bid spades, or to have him pass for penalties. Jump to three clubs with this hand. No matter how you play your *direct* jump overcalls, weak, intermediate or strong, your *balancing* jump overcalls should be of this intermediate strength.

Another special problem is presented by reopening no-trump bids, for you have such a wide range to cover. That is, you should hate to pass out a one-heart opening bid with any of these hands:

(7)   ♠ K 3   ♡ K J 2   ◇ Q 10 9 4   ♣ K 10 8 4
(8)   ♠ A Q   ♡ K J 2   ◇ Q 10 9 4   ♣ K 10 8 4
(9)   ♠ A Q   ♡ K J 2   ◇ A J 9 4   ♣ K 10 8 4

My suggestion is that you reopen with one notrump holding hand (7) (say, 10 to 13 points). Then you can no longer overcall one notrump with hand (8); double and rebid notrump (14 to 16 points). With hand (9), jump directly to two notrump (17 to 19 points).

Finally, there are the hands with which you should not balance at all. Obviously, you will pass when you are very weak (0 to 7) and have no good-looking suit. (Partner should not trap-pass with hands worth 18 points or more; there is no real chance that you can find a reopening double, and a missed game could result.) In addition, be willing to pass out an enemy one-bid even with up to 14 points, when you hold four or five cards in the opponents' suit. Partner is not trapping when you are long in trumps; he passed because he was weak. If you have a fit with your left-hand opponent, the whole deal is probably a mis-fit. Be generous to the enemy—let *them* go down instead of taking a minus yourself.

QUIZ 9

Neither side is vulnerable. The auction goes:

OPENER	PARTNER	RESPONDER	YOU
1 ♡	Pass	Pass	?

What is your action with these hands?

(1) ♠ A Q J 10 8 4 ♡ 2 ◇ K J 8 ♣ J 7 5
(2) ♠ 8 ♡ Q J 8 6 ◇ A Q 4 ♣ K J 8 7 2
(3) ♠ A 10 3 ♡ Q 4 2 ◇ 10 8 7 6 2 ♣ A 5
(4) ♠ K Q 10 7 ♡ 6 ◇ 9 7 5 2 ♣ Q 10 7 4
(5) ♠ K Q J 9 7 ♡ Void ◇ A Q J 10 7 6 ♣ 4 2
(6) ♠ A J 2 ♡ K Q 7 ◇ K 5 ♣ Q 10 9 8 4

Answers

1. *Bid two spades.* You are too strong to overcall, too unbalanced to double.

2. *Pass.* Partner was not strong enough to overcall with one spade. And if he does not have the spades, the opponents do. Take your sure plus.

3. *Bid one notrump.* You do not need magnificent hearts for this overcall; you are bidding because you expect *partner* to hold hearts for his pass.

4. *Bid one spade.* Do not double with so little in high cards. Do not pass when partner may have the best hand at the table.

5. *Bid two hearts.* You dare not double for fear of a penalty pass, and you are too strong for the limited jump overcall.

6. *Double.* You are too strong for one notrump; too weak for two notrump. You will rebid one notrump over a one-spade response, two notrump over two diamonds.

WHEN PARTNER REOPENS

Your right-hand opponent opens with a suit bid, you pass, your left-hand opponent passes also, and partner reopens with a balancing overcall or double. Where do you go from here?

First of all, remember that partner is *expected* to balance—it is most unusual for him to pass. No one ever be-
came a life master by defending against one-bids, so
partner will go out of his way to muster up some action or
other. Thus, you should not do anything violent just because you passed a decent hand. Partner's reopening bid
may have been based on little more than some skinny
spades and a stout heart.

This is particularly true when the balancing bid is an
overcall. Here, partner is unlikely to hold as much as an average hand in high cards, for then he would normally
double. He is bidding on *your* values. So if you hold 10 or
11 points, behave as if you had already shown them. Even
if you have passed a minimum opening hand of 12 to 14
points, there is no real prospect of making a high contract
after partner balances with an overcall. Probably you are
entitled to a plus score, but you will end with a minus if
you go on a big-game hunt. Only if you have trap-passed
with the best hand at the table should you have any high
hopes. And you should rarely leap to game with 15 or 16
points. Unless you have a fit with partner or a wealth of
tenaces behind opener, you must content yourself with an
invitational jump (usually to two notrump).

Here is a deal from a recent tournament:

NORTH

♠ Q 9 2
♡ K 8 5
♢ 9 7 3
♣ A J 7 4

WEST

♠ A 4
♡ A 10 7 6 2
♢ A K 8 2
♣ K 9

EAST

♠ 10 7 6
♡ Q 9 3
♢ J 6 5
♣ Q 10 6 3

SOUTH

♠ K J 8 5 3
♡ J 4
♢ Q 10 4
♣ 8 5 2

West dealer; both vulnerable.

WEST	NORTH	EAST	SOUTH
1 ♡	Pass	Pass	1 ♠
2 ◇	2 ♠	3 ♡	Pass
Pass	Double	Pass	3 ♠
Double	Pass	Pass	Pass

South was lucky to escape for down two, 500. Had he passed the double, as he should, he would probably have scored an even rounder zero: West has only to guess the heart position to make three hearts.

Obviously, North was the culprit. South's balancing overcall had accomplished its purpose—pushing the opponents to a level where they might be beaten. (Incidentally, it directed the best opening lead; left to his own devices, North might open the diamond nine, letting declarer make four or five.) North's raise to two spades was daring enough. He was "rebidding" the values which partner had already bid for him, and could be stung for 200 right there. Clearly, action at the three-level was folly—North should have taken his profit and passed.

When partner reopens with a double, you can be more aggressive. Here too, though, partner may have shaded values, so do not be overanxious to leap about in response. A hand like this one:

♠ Q742　♡ A83　◇ 754　♣ KJ10

is surely worth a jump to two spades if partner doubles *directly* over a one-heart opening. In contrast, I would respond only one spade in answer to a *balancing* double of one heart. Partly this is because partner has not promised good spade support with his reopening double. Partly it is because there is no need to jump; partner is expected to *bid again* if he has a normal, sound double; if he has not, we may be too high at the two-level. There is time enough to try for game after partner rebids.

NOTRUMP RESPONSES

What do notrump bids mean in answer to a balancing double? *One* notrump could be based on anything from a dull 7-point hand up to 10 or 11 points. *Two* notrump means that you passed a minimum opening bid with length in the enemy suit. *Three* notrump is based on a true trap pass of 14 good points or better. Suppose partner doubles a one-spade opening in the reopening position. You hold:

(1)   ♠ Q 10 7 2   ♡ J 8 6 4   ◇ A 7   ♣ J 9 2
(2)   ♠ K Q 8 4   ♡ A 6   ◇ J 8 6 5 3   ♣ Q 5
(3)   ♠ A Q 10 7   ♡ K 5   ◇ K 10 4 2   ♣ Q 8 4

Bid *one* notrump with (1), *two* notrump with (2), and *three* notrump with (3). Of course, you can pass for penalties with either (2) or (3). Vulnerability is a factor in this decision. Nonvulnerable vs. vulnerable, I would pass with either; vulnerable vs. nonvulnerable, with neither. Both vulnerable, I would pass with (2) (game is not sure, and a one-trick or two-trick penalty may be a top) but might bid with (3) (now +200 or +500 rates to be a disaster). With no one vulnerable, I would bid with (2), and probably with (3) as well. When I have to set the opponents *three* tricks at the one-level, I get nervous—it may be too close for comfort. My partners do not always defend accurately; I am happiest when they are dummy. (I don't mean my favorite partners, of course.)

QUIZ 10

You hold, as South, with both sides vulnerable:

♠ A 5   ♡ K J 9 2   ◇ Q 8 4   ♣ 10 7 6 3

What is your call on these auctions?

	EAST	SOUTH	WEST	NORTH
(1)	1 ◇	Pass	Pass	1 ♠
	2 ♣	?		
(2)	1 ♠	Pass	Pass	1 NT
	Pass	?		
(3)	1 ♣	Pass	Pass	Double
	Pass	1 ♡	Pass	1 NT
	Pass	?		

Answers

1. *Pass.* You cannot bid since you have barely the strength partner expects and rather less fit than he hopes for. You have some prospect of defeating an enemy contract, but not enough to double. The opponents have more high-card power than your side has.

2. *Pass.* Partner cannot have the 14 or 15 points you need to give your side a shot at game, for he did not double.

3. *Bid three notrump.* Here, in contrast to the previous problem, partner has enough to put you somewhere in the game range. It is not disgraceful to bid only *two* notrump. However, if partner has 14 points and passes, you will probably make nine or ten tricks anyway. You will console one another by saying that there was no way to bid game with only 24 points, that it was a lucky hand, etc.; but this will earn you no match points. The truth is that deals in which all the enemy high-cards are bottled up in one hand are always lucky. So if you can sniff a game, bid it.

LATER BALANCING

So far, I have treated only one common position for balancing: a one-bid in a suit, opened on your left and passed around to you. The key consideration here—that partner is marked for the "balance" of the strength which the opponents' auction denies—can apply as well to many situations on the second or even third round of bidding.

For example, consider this sequence:

OPENER	YOU	RESPONDER	PARTNER
1 ♡	Pass	2 ♡	Pass
Pass	?		

An experienced duplicate player will reopen with a balancing overcall or double more than three times out of four in this position. Why? First, because the opponents have found a fit. If they have a fit the odds are great that you have one too. Second, because they have stopped short despite their fit; clearly, they do not have a preponderance of high cards—your side has nearly half the deck.

Third, because minus 110 usually results in a filthy match-point score; if you can push the enemy to the three-level you may get a plus, and you need pluses to do well at duplicate.

Suppose your hand, on the auction above, is:

♠ 9 7 6 5 3   ♡ J 4   ◇ A K 10 2   ♣ 9 7

Bid two spades. Partner must have considerable strength (probably 10 points or more); he is likely to fit spades; you will not get rich defending against two hearts. The whole deal probably is much like this:

NORTH
♠ A 10 2
♡ Q 8 6
◇ Q 9 3
♣ K 10 5 4

WEST
♠ Q 8 4
♡ A 9 2
◇ 8 7 6 4
♣ J 3 2

EAST
♠ K J
♡ K 10 7 5 3
◇ J 5
♣ A Q 8 6

SOUTH
♠ 9 7 6 5 3
♡ J 4
◇ A K 10 2
♣ 9 7

East-West can make two hearts; North-South are down one at most in two spades (they might even make it). And the most likely result of the two-spade balancing over-call is for East to bid three hearts and go down one. Note that South was not just lucky to find partner with all those cards. Try to take away the spade ace from North and give it to an opponent: West would be too strong for a single raise; East would have a solid game try over the raise. Nor is it dumb luck to find partner with three spades. If the enemy have an eight-card fit, you are an overwhelming favorite to have one yourself; if they have a nine-card fit, you and partner *must* have a fit somewhere. The fact is that if I were South I would be mildly disappointed in North's hand. But then, I am an optimist.

What if the North-South hands were reversed? That is, the auction goes one heart, pass, two hearts, pass, pass, to you when you hold:

♠ A 10 2   ♡ Q 8 6   ◇ Q 9 3   ♣ K 10 5 4

Double. Despite a respectable point count, your flat distribution kept you out of the auction earlier. But now that the opponents have found a fit, the odds favor your having one too. This reopening double is simply a balancing overcall in partner's best suit. If the deal is the same, partner will bid two spades (and this time you can make your contract). However, the probable result, as before, is three hearts down one.

Be sure that you understand that these delayed balancing sequences are odds-on to work only when the opponents have found a fit. Suppose that you hold this earlier example hand:

♠ 9 7 6 5 3   ♡ J 4   ◇ A K 10 2   ♣ 9 7

This time, though, the auction goes:

OPENER	PARTNER	RESPONDER	YOU
1 ♡	Pass	2 ♣	Pass
2 ♡	Pass	Pass	?

Do not dream of balancing—just pass. Here, there is no reason to expect partner to hold either a decent hand or a fit with you. The opponents have stopped short not so much because of a lack of points as because of a misfit. So you probably have a misfit too. And partner has a poorer hand than you have. It is unpleasant to let the opponents play at the two-level, but you will enjoy a 500-point set even less.

Vulnerability should not much affect your decision whether to balance. True, vulnerable balancing bids will earn you an occasional minus 200. Do not write to me and complain—I have gone for numbers, too. In the long run, you will show a big profit from reopening at the two-level after the opponents have found a fit. Of course, you are more nervous when vulnerable. But balance anyway—and in an even firmer tone of voice.

QUIZ 11

1. You are South, nonvulnerable, on this auction:

WEST	NORTH	EAST	SOUTH
1 ♣	Pass	1 ♡	Pass
2 ♡	Pass	Pass	?

What is your action with these hands?

(a) ♠ Q 8 2   ♡ J 6 4 3   ◇ A 10 8 4   ♣ A 9
(b) ♠ K Q   ♡ 6   ◇ Q 9 7 4 2   ♣ J 10 9 5 2

2. You are South, both vulnerable, on this auction:

EAST	SOUTH	WEST	NORTH
1 ♡	Pass	1 NT	Pass
Pass	?		

What is your action with these hands?

(c) ♠ K 7 4 3   ♡ 10 7 3   ◇ A J 3   ♣ K 4 2
(d) ♠ K 3   ♡ 4   ◇ Q 10 9 8 6 4   ♣ J 10 7 5

Answers

a. *Double.* The opponents have found a fit, so try to push them to the three-level, where they may be beaten.

b. *Bid two notrump.* This is, of course, the "unusual no-trump." The reasons for balancing are the same as in (a) —after an enemy raise, fight them to the three-level.

c. *Pass.* Here the opponents have *not* found a fit, so there is no presumption that *you* have one. In fact, a double here is *not* a balancing bid at all. It means that you were trapping over one heart, and is for penalties.

d. *Bid two diamonds.* You cannot expect partner to fit diamonds, but you do not need much trump support. You need high cards, and partner surely has them. (The opponents have 23 or 24 points at most, so partner has 10 or 11 at least.)

VI. BATTLING OVER PART SCORES

The experienced match-point player loves part-score hands. When one side has most of the high cards, the bidding decisions—whether to go to game, whether to try for slam—are simple and clear-cut. The pro has little advantage; a club rubber-bridge player, an earnest point counter, or even an IBM machine might do as well. In contrast, when neither side has the power to bid game, judgment, not arithmetic, is called for. The auction is often a wild scramble, and the seasoned duplicate player usually emerges from the melee with most of the match points.

FIT OR MISFIT?

Here, the decisions to be made are (1) whether to let the opponents play the hand or to outbid them, and (2) if you do let them buy the hand, whether to double. One prime consideration in answering the first question is whether the deal is a misfit or good-fitting. That is, on many deals each side has a good trump suit and a little distributional value. Then, if there is no preponderance of strength, either side can win about eight tricks; it is advantageous to buy the contract. Occasionally, though, neither side has a good trump suit, everyone has a fit with an opponent (partner bids your singleton, or your opponent bids your five-card suit). Now no one can make much and you should generally allow the enemy to struggle with the misfit and go down.

For example, suppose that you hold:

♠ Q 10 7 3   ♡ J 8 6 4 3   ◇ 4   ♣ A 7 5

PARTNER	OPPONENT	YOU	OPPONENT
1 ◇	1 ♠	Pass	2 ♣
Pass	Pass	?	

Do not bid two hearts—let them buy the hand. All the danger signals are flying: length in an enemy suit, short-

ness in partner's, an auction in which the opponents have
not supported one another.

Do not dream of selling out, though, if the auction was:

OPPONENT	YOU	OPPONENT	PARTNER
1 ◊	Pass	2 ◊	Pass
Pass	?		

Here, the deal is a good fit all around, so get in there and
fight.

WHO OWNS THE HAND?

Of course, you cannot insist stubbornly on playing all
good-fitting hands your way, regardless of level. If both
sides can make eight tricks, it pays to give up at the
three-level. If your side can make nine tricks only, you
would prefer not to fight up to four. It can yield a decent
score to go down one trick rather than let the opponents
make a partial. But it is better still to be plus.

On these deals, the major consideration is: *Who owns
the hand?* You must learn to distinguish among three tactical positions. (1) They own the hand, with about 23
high-card points to your 17. Your sole objective is a small
minus, or conceivably a plus, if you can push the opponents to the three-level where they may go down. (2)
The high cards are evenly split, and it is nobody's hand.
Your objective is primarily any plus score. (3) Your side
owns the majority of points. Your objective is the largest
plus score possible.

THEIR HAND

First, let us examine an auction in which you are outgunned:

OPPONENT	PARTNER	OPPONENT	YOU
1 ♡	Pass	2 ♡	Pass
Pass	2 ♠	Pass	Pass
3 ♡	Pass	Pass	?

You hold, with no one vulnerable:

♠ K ͺ5 ♡ K 10 7 2 ◇ K 6 4 3 ♣ 8 6

Should you bid three spades or double three hearts? No; you should pass! To be sure, it is possible that three hearts will be beaten; it is possible that three spades will be down only one trick for a good score. It would be a different tactical position entirely if partner had acted directly over one heart. But when he has merely balanced, they own the hand, so your side need do nothing radical. Partner may hold:

♠ Q 10 9 4 ♡ 6 ◇ J 8 2 ♣ A 10 6 3 2

Note that he was bidding your cards when he balanced; you must avoid rebidding the same values. If you beat three hearts, partner's enterprise will be rewarded with a big match-point score, while if the contract makes, you will be close to average. However, if you double or bid, you may punish partner's daring with a zero.

The essential point is that the balancing bid has already accomplished your objective on deals they own: pushing them to the three-level. You have a fighting chance for a plus score against the cards. (This is analogous to the situation in which you sacrifice against an enemy four-heart contract, and they go on to five.) You do not need a great big score—any plus is magnificent.

So take your profit and pass.

QUIZ 12

You are South, with no one vulnerable, holding:

♠ A J 7 2 ♡ J 8 ◇ 9 3 ♣ Q 10 7 6 4

What do you do on these auctions?

	EAST	SOUTH	WEST	NORTH
(1)	1 ♡	Pass	Pass	1 ♠
	2 ♡	2 ♠	3 ♡	Pass
	Pass	?		

	EAST	SOUTH	WEST	NORTH
(2)	Pass	Pass	1 ◇	Double
	1 ♡	1 ♠	2 ◇	2 ♠
	Pass	Pass	3 ◇	Pass
	Pass	?		
(3)	1 ♣	Pass	1 ◇	1 ♡
	1 NT	Pass	2 ◇	Pass
	Pass	?		

Answers

1. *Pass.* This is their hand, since partner reopened with an overcall; your side has about 17 points at most. Thanks to partner, you can defend against *three* hearts instead of *one* heart.

2. *Bid three spades.* Here, this may be your hand; partner likely has about 14 points to add to your 8. Note the difference in objective—you are trying to make something yourself, not merely to push the enemy up.

3. *Pass.* This looks like "nobody's" hand. The high cards are evenly divided and no one has much of a fit with partner. Do not fight fiercely to buy yourself trouble on misfit hands. (Besides, if you bid two hearts you will be dummy, while if you pass, your magnificent defensive technique can be brought into play.)

NOBODY'S HAND

Up to now we have been selling out timidly on misfit hands, or on deals in which the enemy have the clear majority of the points and are pushed to the three-level. On good-fitting deals in which your side has its fair share of cards, you can be more pugnacious.

The trickiest decisions must be made when each partnership has close to 20 high-card points, a good trump suit and a little distribution. For example:

SOUTH	WEST	NORTH	EAST
1 ♣	Double	1 ♡	1 ♠
2 ♡	2 ♠		

North-South have an opening bid opposite a minimum

response; East-West have a double opposite a free response. Neither side has the balance of power. The simple rules for this sort of deal are (1) do not sell out at the two-level, and (2) never go to the four-level without magnificent distribution. It is the three-level which is the battleground. Suppose that this is the full deal:

NORTH

♠ 10 2
♡ Q J 9 8 4
◇ 8 5 4
♣ A 7 2

WEST

♠ A J 8 5
♡ K 7 2
◇ K Q 10 6
♣ 4 3

EAST

♠ K Q 7 6 3
♡ 6 5
◇ J 9
♣ J 10 9 5

SOUTH

♠ 9 4
♡ A 10 3
◇ A 7 3 2
♣ K Q 8 6

Notice two things about this unspectacular example. First, no one at the table could possibly tell during the auction, or even after seeing partner's hand, which side owned the hand: who is bidding for a make and who for a sacrifice. (As it is, North-South can make two hearts, East-West three spades. But if the heart finesse worked for North-South, then *they* could make three, the enemy only two.) This means that no one can conveniently double a three-level contract.

Second, regardless of the position of the heart ace or king, it is correct for each side to bid as high as three of its suit. With the heart king onside, North-South could make three hearts; with it offside, they are better off down one in three hearts than defending against two spades. Likewise, East-West must gain by bidding three spades—depending on the position of the heart ace, they will have a make or a good sacrifice.

However, you must not *always* compete at the three-level on this type of deal. Suppose that you are West, holding:

♠ A 9 8 6 4 ♡ Q J 5 ◇ A 8 3 ♣ 7 2

The auction goes:

SOUTH	WEST	NORTH	EAST
1 ♡	1 ♠	2 ♡	2 ♠
Pass	Pass	3 ♡	Pass
Pass	?		

Even though this is "nobody's" hand and both sides have a fit, you should pass. The key factor is third-round trump winners. Here, you have the heart queen, a trick on defense but no help in a spade contract. You are missing the intermediates in your own suit, no hindrance on defense against hearts but a serious danger in spades. If partner holds:

♠ K 10 2 ♡ 6 3 ◇ K Q 9 7 4 ♣ 1 0 8 4

the limit for either side is probably eight tricks. Whoever *sells out* at the three-level will win the match points.

Of course, your distribution is a big factor too. If your pattern is 4–3–3–3, you should be much more willing to give up at the three-level. And if you have a singleton, you should bid up to three regardless of intermediates. For instance, either example hand above should compete with three spades over three hearts if its doubleton were, instead, a singleton.

Here, then, are the policies I recommend when the high cards are equally divided and both sides have a fit:

1. Normally, compete as high as three in your own suit.
2. Let the opponents play at the three-level if you have flat distribution, or have strong intermediates in their suit and weak ones in your own.
3. Do not sell out at two; do not compete up to four.

And remember, for goodness' sake, that these are vague policies, not hard-and-fast rules. Violate them whenever you feel like it. But you had better be right when you do.

QUIZ 13

1. You are South on the auction below:

NORTH	EAST	SOUTH	WEST
1 ◇	Double	Pass	1 ♡
1 ♠	2 ♡	2 ♠	3 ♡
Pass	Pass	?	

What is your action with these hands?

(a)   ♠ Q J 10 4   ♡ A 8 2   ◇ 9 4   ♣ 9 8 6 2

(b)   ♠ A 7 4 3   ♡ J 9 4   ◇ 8 6 5   ♣ Q J 8

2. You are South on this auction:

NORTH	EAST	SOUTH	WEST
1 ♡	1 ♠	2 ◇	2 ♠
3 ◇	Pass	Pass	3 ♠
Pass	Pass	?	

What is your action, holding:

(c)   ♠ 3   ♡ K 7   ◇ K Q 9 8 5 2   ♣ 8 6 4 3

(d)   ♠ 8 5 3   ♡ 7 4   ◇ A Q 9 6 4   ♣ K Q 6

Answers

a. *Bid three spades.* This is "nobody's" hand, and both sides have a fit. Compete at the three-level when you have neither third-round losers in your suit nor third-round winners in theirs.

b. *Pass.* The differences here are (1) your flat distribution, (2) the possibility of third-round losers in spades or diamonds, (3) your good chance for third-round winners in hearts and clubs. The outstanding prospect for a plus score is to sell out at the three-level.

c. *Bid four diamonds.* It is seldom right to compete up to the four-level when your side has only half the high cards. All three of these conditions must be present: exciting distribution; no wasted honors in the enemy suits; no danger of third-round losers in your suits.

d. *Double*. Do you see what is different about this example? Here, your side has considerably more than half the high-card strength; it is your hand, not "nobody's" hand. As we will see in the following section, it is necessary to be greedy when you own the hand.

YOUR HAND

So far, we have covered two of the common positions in the duplicate dogfight over part-score deals: (1) when the opponents have the clear majority of high cards, and your object is merely to push them to the three-level; (2) when the cards are evenly divided, and you will take your best combined chance for any plus score or for a small minus. Now, we will examine objectives and tactics when your side has substantially more power than have the opponents.

If your partnership has 23 or 24 high-card points to 16 or 17 for the enemy, you must assume that nearly every pair sitting your way will be plus. This means that you are in grave jeopardy in contested auctions. A minus score will yield close to 0 match points; a small plus score (50 or 100) may be substantially under average. You must fight fiercely for the biggest plus possible.

For example, suppose that you hold, with no one vulnerable:

♠ K Q 10 6 3   ♡ 8 4   ◇ J 7   ♣ J 9 5 2

The auction goes:

PARTNER	OPPONENT	YOU	OPPONENT
1 NT	Pass	2 ♠	Pass
Pass	Double	Pass	3 ◇
Pass	Pass	?	

If partner's opening shows 12 to 14 points, you should pass. This is "nobody's" hand, so you need not strain for a big plus. Maybe three diamonds will go down; maybe the opponents could make more playing in hearts. And even if three diamonds is the perfect spot for the enemy, you will score about 30 percent on the board.

In contrast, if partner's opening shows 16 to 18 points you should not dream of passing—you must double. This is your hand, and if the opponents want to buy it you must try to make them pay a stiff price. True, you are not at all sure of setting three diamonds; but you are confident of making two spades. This means that if three diamonds makes against you *undoubled*, you will score barely 10 percent on the board—if three diamonds makes *doubled*, the double costs little. What is more, you will have a poor score if you set three diamonds one or two tricks undoubled. Down one doubled will be no bonanza either, but there is an outside chance for down two. Then your double will gain heavily, converting a 30 percent board into a top.

Treat "your" part-score hands the same way you do your game deals: that is, if the opponents sacrifice, they must never be allowed to play undoubled; you will either bid one more or double. In the example above, you cannot think seriously about bidding on to three spades, for the deal could be a misfit. Sometimes, though, the decision may be a close one.

Suppose you hold:

♠ A J 7 5 3   ♡ 6 2   ◇ K 8 4 3   ♣ K Q

The auction goes:

YOU	OPPONENT	PARTNER	OPPONENT
1 ♠	Pass	2 ◇	2 ♡
3 ◇	3 ♡	Pass	Pass
?			

Partner's pass over three hearts is a forcing pass (just as if you bid game and they sacrificed); with an opening bid opposite a two-over-one response, it is your hand. So you must double or bid four diamonds. Which?

You rate to beat three hearts, but you might not; partner figures to make four diamonds, but there is a clear danger of four losers. In these touch-and-go positions, I suggest that you decide according to the opponents' vulnerability. If they are vulnerable, double—you risk a zero, but are odds-on to collect 200 for a near-top. If they are nonvulnerable, bid four diamonds—now, a one-trick penalty against three hearts doubled will be under average, so try for a decent result by bidding on. The whole deal may be:

NORTH
♠ K 9
♡ Q 5
◇ A J 10 9 2
♣ 7 6 5 3

WEST
♠ Q 8 6 4
♡ K 8 4
◇ Q 7 5
♣ J 9 2

EAST
♠ 10 2
♡ A J 10 9 7 3
◇ 6
♣ A 10 8 4

SOUTH
♠ A J 7 5 3
♡ 6 2
◇ K 8 4 3
♣ K Q

Note that East can make three hearts by guessing both hearts and clubs, but will usually go down one. North can make four diamonds if he guesses the trump position, but is by no means certain to do so.

If you bid four diamonds, your match points will average slightly under 50 percent. Sometimes the contract will make for a good score; sometimes it will go down for a horrible result (many North-South pairs will buy this hand at three diamonds). True, you and I would always guess the trump queen on this auction, but partner is declarer, remember.

If you double three hearts, your match points will average about 30 percent when East-West are nonvulnerable. (You will usually get +100 for a moderately poor score, occasionally −470 for a zero, rarely +300 for a top.) When East-West are vulnerable, you will average over 70 percent (usually +200, occasionally −670, rarely +500).

If you pass three hearts, you will always get the score you deserve. I'd love to play against you some time.

QUIZ 14

West is dealer; only East-West are vulnerable. You are South. On the following auctions, what is your call with this hand?

♠ Q96   ♡ 10872   ◇ AQ65   ♣ J2

	WEST	NORTH	EAST	SOUTH
(1)	1 ♡	Pass	2 ♡	Pass
	Pass	2 ♠	Pass	Pass
	3 ♡	Pass	Pass	?
(2)	1 ♡	1 ♠	2 ♡	2 ♠
	3 ♡	Pass	Pass	?
(3)	Pass	1 ♠	Pass	2 ♠
	Pass	Pass	Double	Pass
	3 ♡	Pass	Pass	?

Answers

1. *Pass.* This is their hand, for partner could not act immediately. If you bid three spades, you rate to be doubled and set 300. Do not double them on their own hand. You do not need to risk a zero trying to get a 200 number, since +100 your way will be a magnificent score. And if three hearts makes, as it usually will, you will be close to average.

2. *Bid three spades.* This gives you two chances for a good score—either that three spades will make, or that it is down one when three hearts was a make. On a hand that is owned by neither side, it usually pays to compete up to three when you have found a fit. Since the opponents are vulnerable, it could be right to double; when the cards lie favorably for your side, you will earn 200 instead of 140. But this is a blind gamble against the odds. You have no reason to expect favorable breaks; and when they exist, your score for bidding three spades will be handsomely over average anyway.

3. *Double*. Do you see the difference between this auction and the previous one? Here, it is *your* hand; probably half the pairs your way are playing peacefully in two spades and making 110 or 140. So it is much more dangerous to bid three spades—if you go down, you will get a filthy score even if three hearts could make, while if you make three spades, you will be only slightly over average. Your best bet, since the opponents are vulnerable, is to shoot for a top by doubling.

VII. PENALTY DOUBLES

The whole area of penalty doubles abounds in strictly
"duplicate" positions. This is because any decision to
double has a mathematical foundation: "How much can I
lose?" compared with "What have I to gain?" When loss
and gain are converted from total points to match points,
the odds change, usually drastically.

We have already seen this in the double of enemy part
scores when you have been outbid on "your own" hand.
That is, the double which produces a 200 set gains only
100 total points but perhaps as many as 10 additional
match points (on a 12 top). And when the double gives
the opponents 730, the extra 590 total points often costs
no more than 2 match points. Here, total-point odds of 6
to 1 against doubling have changed into match-point odds
of 5 to 1 in favor.

DOUBLING A SACRIFICE

Let us look at the odds involved in the most common
doubling decision. The opponents have sacrificed against
your game contract; should you double them or bid one
more yourself? Obviously, you or partner will double if
you have stretched to bid game and have little prospect
of making more. And it is not difficult to bid on when
either of you has so much extra strength as to provide
complete safety at a higher level. But usually the decision
will be a ticklish affair. Suppose that you hold:

♠ K 10 7 2   ♡ 5 3   ◇ A 10 9 6 3   ♣ 9 4

You are second hand, with no one vulnerable, and the
auction goes:

OPPONENT	YOU	OPPONENT	PARTNER
Pass	Pass	3 ♡	3 ♠
4 ♡	4 ♠	5 ♡	Pass
Pass	?		

There is no assurance that you can make five spades, since you have neither freakish distribution nor great high-card strength (if you had a singleton heart and three clubs, it would be clear to bid on). However, your hand is better for attack than for defense, and there must be a reasonable shot to make five spades. Partner would have doubled himself, instead of passing, if he had minimum values, and you might well have bid four spades with less (if your diamond ace were the queen, it would be clear to double). Well, partner's pass is forcing after an enemy sacrifice. Do you bid a risky five spades, or settle for a likely 300 penalty by doubling five hearts?

The odds favor doubling. If you bid five spades, you risk a zero for going down, and, in return for this risk, will score only a little over average for making your contract—most pairs will buy the hand for *four* spades and tie you. In contrast, you will score a few points anyway for setting five hearts 300, and have a fighting chance for a top by collecting 500. So although you are a little more likely to make five spades than to collect 500, you will earn more match points in the long run by doubling. Here is the full deal:

NORTH
♠ K 10 7 2
♡ 5 3
♢ A 10 9 6 3
♣ 9 4

WEST
♠ 8 5
♡ K 7 6
♢ Q J 8 4
♣ K 8 6 5

EAST
♠ 4
♡ A Q J 10 9 4
♢ 7 2
♣ J 10 7 3

SOUTH
♠ A Q J 9 6 3
♡ 8 2
♢ K 5
♣ A Q 2

South is certainly justified in passing five hearts around

to partner, for he has considerable extra strength. Yet five spades has little better than a 50 percent chance, and would here be a disastrous contract.

What if East held the club king? Then five spades would make (for a fair match-point result); but then five hearts would be set 500, for a top. Actually, there is a chance for 500 even as the cards lie, for East may misguess in clubs.

The time to push on to five of your suit is when you are morally certain of making. This means that both partners have tiptop maximums; in the example above, South has one, but North has not. Otherwise, shoot for a top by doubling, rather than settle for the average-or-zero position at the five-level.

The odds are different when you have no hope to defeat the sacrifice by more than the value of your game. Usually, this is true when the vulnerability is unfavorable; occasionally, it is because your values are strictly offensive. Here, you should double only when you believe that you have little chance to make five, and bid on if you have a decent prospect. That is, only one partner need have extra values.

Remember, though, that sacrifice bids have been known to be set 700. Nonvulnerable opponents sometimes get very frisky when you are vulnerable. So if your extra values are high honors in side suits or in the enemy suit, a double may be your best bet.

QUIZ 15

You are South, holding:

♠ Q 6 4 2   ♡ Q 7 6   ◇ A 10 8 4 2   ♣ 5

What is your call on the following auctions?

1. No one vulnerable

EAST	NORTH	WEST	SOUTH
1 ♡	1 ♠	3 ♡	4 ♠
5 ♡	Pass	Pass	?

2. North-South vulnerable.

EAST	NORTH	WEST	SOUTH
Pass	1 ♡	Double	2 ♡
3 ♣	4 ♡	Pass	Pass
4 ♠	Pass	Pass	?

3. North-South vulnerable.

EAST	NORTH	WEST	SOUTH
Pass	1 ♠		Pass
Pass	4 ♠	2 ♣	3 ♠
5 ♣	Pass	Pass	Pass
		Pass	?

4. North-South vulnerable.

EAST	NORTH	WEST	SOUTH
Pass	1 ♠		Pass
Pass	4 ♣	Pass	3 ♠
5 ♣	Pass	Double	4 ♠
		Pass	?

Answers

1. *Pass.* This is not the position in which partner's pass is forcing on you. *They* have not sacrificed; *you* have. Never double the opponents (and seldom bid on) when your sacrifice has pushed them to the five-level.

2. *Bid five hearts or five diamonds.* You certainly have a supermaximum for your timid raise to two hearts, so if partner can invite five hearts by passing, the contract must be laydown. Even slam is possible.

3. *Double.* You have a skinny minimum for your jump raise, and so must decline partner's invitation. You will not beat five clubs enough to make up for game, but at least you will be plus. On this vulnerability, many other East-West pairs will save, so you may be only a little under average for plus 300.

4. *Bid five spades.* This looks like the same situation as in (3), but there is a big difference. The opponents got into the auction only by a fluke; almost all the other pairs your

way will buy the contract for four spades. Thus, plus 300 or 500 will get the same zero as minus 100. When you think that your opponents have taken a most unusual sacrifice, you cannot afford to double unless you hope to set them more than the value of your game. Even when you have little hope of making five, you should bid on. You might as well take your bottom fighting.

DOUBLING AN OVERCALL

The experienced rubber-bridge player loves to double overcalls. When he has 10 points or more opposite partner's opening bid, and his right-hand opponent climbs into the auction, he will double any time he has a smattering of strength in the enemy suit and no great fit with partner's. (He is not worried about collecting only 300 or 500 in place of a nonvulnerable or vulnerable game; he is after the sure profit, the "money in the bank.") In addition, he may double with much weaker hands when he has five good trumps behind the overcaller. (He is not concerned lest partner or an opponent run to another suit; he is after a big plus, a bonanza.)

However, match-point scoring changes the odds so drastically that your attitude toward doubling overcalls must be entirely different. The bonanza double, based on long trumps and nothing else, is ridiculous: down three or four undoubled (a score that would nauseate a rubber-bridge player) will probably be close to a top, so it is silly to double and warn the opponents to run; and if your side has a game, so that it is necessary to collect a big number, partner will reopen with a takeout double which you can convert with a penalty pass.

The double based on high cards plus fair length and strength in the enemy suit is possible at duplicate, but it can be very dangerous. If this "money-in-the-bank" double collects 500, it may earn not a nest-egg but a goose-egg, if everyone else is making a vulnerable game. The overriding factor here is the vulnerability. Therefore, I will discuss the four conditions of vulnerability separately. In all examples below, assume that the auction has been:

PARTNER	OPPONENT	YOU	OPPONENT
1 ♡	2 ◇	?	

NONVULNERABLE VS. VULNERABLE: This, of course, is where you make your hungry doubles; a two-trick set will be a top, and even a one-trick set will be magnificent if you have no game. Double, holding:

(1)   ♠ A K 7 2   ♡ 6 3   ◊ Q 10 5   ♣ Q 9 7 3
(2)   ♠ K J 8 5 2   ♡ 2   ◊ J 8 3   ♣ A Q 6 4

The important features are high-card strength and shortness in hearts. The shorter you are in partner's suit, the less you need in the enemy suit to double. Holding:

(3)   ♠ A 8 6   ♡ K J 5 2   ◊ A 7 4 2   ♣ 9 5
(4)   ♠ A 8 6 2   ♡ K Q 5   ◊ Q J 4 2   ♣ 9 5

Do not double with (3). Your hearts are so good that game is sure; now that you surely need 500, your diamonds are too weak, particularly since your honor there is as useful on attack as on defense. Double with (4), since your diamonds are better on attack, and more of a nasty surprise for declarer.

VULNERABLE VS. VULNERABLE: Here, you need a three-trick set to compensate for game, but a one-trick set will beat any part-score result. So, what are your chances for game? With misfits like (1) and (2) above, the double is still attractive; less so on (2) since there may be game in spades. It is inconceivable to double with (3), and probably unwise even with (4)—your fit with partner is too good. Make speculative doubles when short in partner's suit, but not with three-card or longer support.

NONVULNERABLE VS. NONVULNERABLE: Again you must defeat a contract three if you have game, but now you must set it two if you have a part score. So, how good are your trumps?

(5)   ♠ A J 4   ♡ 8 2   ◊ K J 9 2   ♣ K 7 4 3
(6)   ♠ A J 8 4   ♡ 2   ◊ Q 10 9 4   ♣ K 10 5 3

These are sound doubles (as compared with (1) and (2) which are not) on this vulnerability: (5) has good enough trumps to promise 500; (6) has prospects of 500, but, equally important, may not produce game because of the misfit.

VULNERABLE VS. NONVULNERABLE: Since either a three-trick set (when you have game) or a one-trick set (when you have a part score) can be a disaster, you double only when you expect a two-trick set: you have good trumps and remote game prospects. Of the previous examples, only hand (6) qualifies. And when you double, partner must be alert to take out if he considers game likely; that is, if he holds the high-card strength to produce three no-trump, or a second long suit.

QUIZ 16

Partner opens the bidding with one spade, your right-hand opponent overcalls with two hearts. What is your action on each of the four vulnerability conditions with these hands?

(1) ♠ 8 6   ♥ K 10 2   ♦ A J 5 4   ♣ K 7 5 3
(2) ♠ 2   ♥ K J 10 8 3   ♦ Q 7 5 4 2   ♣ 7 4
(3) ♠ A 9 6 2   ♥ A J 8 7 2   ♦ K 3   ♣ 6 3

Answers

1. *Double* happily if nonvulnerable vs. vulnerable; *double* even when vulnerable vs. vulnerable, since game is by no means odds-on, and 200 may be a top. However, *bid two notrump* nonvulnerable vs. nonvulnerable (and certainly vulnerable vs. nonvulnerable); there is danger of collecting only 100 for a zero.

2. *Pass* on all vulnerabilities. You can ask nothing better than that the opponents stay right where they are. If partner reopens with a double, you will again decline to disturb the contract.

3. *Double* when nonvulnerable vs. vulnerable. On all other vulnerabilities, *make a forcing jump in spades* instead. You have much too good a fit with partner to gamble on beating the opponents three (or, certainly, four); you know that you have game. If the heart ace were the queen, you would have a better double.

DOUBLING A GAME OR SLAM

Your opponents creep up to a game contract after a labored auction in which, it sounds to you, both have stretched their values. You hold a few defensive tricks, and it looks to you as if the whole hand is breaking unfavorably for declarer; should you double? In rubber bridge, *yes*. Particularly if the opponents are vulnerable, you stand to gain a little more than you might lose, and you will defeat the contract more than half the time. But in duplicate, *no*. The match-point odds are far too unfavorable.

If the contract can be made despite the bad breaks, then you were wrong about the limited sound of the auction; the opponents have bid a sound game which everyone else will bid too, and your double costs 5 or 6 match points on a 12 top. However, if you were right in your feeling that the opponents were overbidding and you beat them two, your double does not gain very much. You were going to score 9 or 10 match points anyway for defeating the contract undoubled; your double is worth only 2 or 3 extra points. The odds against the double are 2 to 1, and this does not allow for the complete disaster that you suffer when declarer makes his contract *because* you have doubled it.

The only occasions on which it is necessary to double voluntarily bid contracts are those that spell trouble for *all* the players who hold the enemy cards, not just for your opponents who bid too much. For example, there is the typical misfit auction:

NORTH	SOUTH
1 ♠	2 ♦
2 ♡	3 ♣
3 ♡	4 ♣
4 ♠	

Every North-South pair in the room might be minus on these cards, so if you are sitting East or West you must be alert to double for a big plus. The same could be true of a more normal auction like this one:

NORTH	SOUTH
1 ♠	2 ◇
2 ♠	4 ♠

Suppose that you are East, sitting behind declarer with:

♠ Q J 10 9 4   ♡ A 8 5   ◇ 6 4   ♣ J 8 2

By all means, double. One time in ten, declarer may make his doubled contract (he is void in hearts, or he endplays you in trumps). But nine times out of ten he goes down like everyone else, and you will not enjoy your score for +50 when all the other East-Wests get +100.

The same reasoning can apply to a *slam* contract. Suppose that on this auction:

NORTH	SOUTH
1 ♠	3 ♠
4 NT	5 ◇
6 ♠	

you are sitting East, behind the spade bidder, holding:

♠ K 6   ♡ A 10 6 2   ◇ 8 7 4 2   ♣ 10 8 5

You should double. This would be foolish at rubber bridge, for you cannot gain enough compared with what you can lose. But at duplicate, you reflect that the auction sounds rather normal—it might be repeated at many other tables. If you score +100 when six other pairs get +50, your double has gained 3 match points. If the ace of trumps is behind you, your double has cost 3 match points. And it is a lot better than an even-money bet that North has the ace of spades.

Most slam doubles, of course, are used to call for a specific opening lead. These lead-directing doubles are magnificently odds-on at rubber bridge, and they are at duplicate too. The point is that any slam your opponents reach is likely to be an unusual contract; if it is made against you, you will have a very poor score. Thus, if it is made doubled, you have lost very few match points by doubling. When you take a chance and double in order to increase your prospect of defeating the slam (not to increase the size of the penalty), you risk 2 points to gain 10.

The same is not true of the lead-directing double of three notrump. There is no more normal contract in all of duplicate than three notrump (when your opponents have the bulk of the cards). Thus, a double risks not 2 points but 6 points. You can double on speculation in rubber bridge, but, at match points, the lead you direct had better defeat the contract. Or start running!

QUIZ 17

You are South, holding:

♠ Q J 10 8 ♡ A 2 ◇ 6 3 ♣ K 8 5 3 2

Do you double, or not, on the following auctions?

	WEST	NORTH	EAST	SOUTH
(1)	1 ♠	Pass	1 NT	Pass
	2 ♠	Pass	3 ♠	Pass
	4 ♠	Pass	Pass	?
(2)	1 ♠	Pass	3 ♠	Pass
	4 ♠	Pass	Pass	?
(3)	1 ♠	Pass	2 ◇	Pass
	2 ♠	Pass	3 ♣	Pass
	3 NT	Pass	6 NT	?
(4)	1 ♡	Pass	2 ♣	Pass
	3 ◇	Pass	4 ♣	Pass
	4 NT	Pass	5 ◇	Pass
	6 NT	Pass	Pass	?

Answers

1. *Pass.* Of course the contract will go down more often than it will make. But the contract sounds unusual, so you gain very little by doubling when you set them; you lose a lot when they make. And they are more likely to make if you double.

2. *Double*. Here, everyone else is in game too, running into the same bad breaks as your opponents. Since the contract sounds normal, so that your double can gain a lot, take a chance.

3. *Pass*. Of course, the opponents are probably bidding wildly and will go down. But then you have a top anyway. A double will make you *less* likely, not more likely, to defeat the abnormal slam.

4. *Double*. This slam sounds abnormal also, but now your double—calling for a club lead—greatly increases your chances of defeating the contract. You were headed for a zero anyway if declarer has the guarded ace of clubs, so the double is "free."

VIII. TEAM-OF-FOUR TACTICS

The scoring of team-of-four contests is so unlike that of match-point pair games that a different set of bidding tactics is required. In this chapter, I will concentrate on these differences: how you must change your match-point style in order to play teams.

There are three important scoring methods for team contests. The simplest is **total points**; however, this is rarely used nowadays except in home games, so I will not discuss it here. The two methods which are commonly used are called **board-a-match** and **international match points** (IMPs).

BOARD-A-MATCH: Your result is computed on each deal separately; that is, the team's North-South and East-West results are added. If your team is *plus*, no matter how much, you score 1 point; if the result is zero (both tables have the same result) you score ½ point; if you are minus (10 total points or 1,000 total points), you score nothing.

IMP'S: Again, your team's North-South and East-West results are added on each separate deal. If you have a plus of more than 10 total points, you will be plus some number of international match points. The bigger your plus, the more imps you earn, but on a sliding scale (for example, +20 total points is +1 imp; +200 total points is +5 imps; +2,000 total points is +19 imps). If you are minus, the result is converted into imps for your opponents (or minus imps for you—it is the same thing). And a standoff on a deal scores zero.

Board-a-match scoring is customarily used for multiple team contests. Many teams enter an event, usually of two sessions; each team plays twenty-four rounds of two boards each against twenty-four different teams (these figures may vary slightly). At the end, each team adds up its points won—the highest score determines the winner of the event.

In contrast, IMP scoring is used for long head-on

matches, team against team. Thirty-two boards may be played—at the end of them, the teams add up their imps, plus and minus. The team which is plus wins, and remains in the competition; the loser is knocked out. Eventually, only two teams are left, and they play each other for the championship.

BOARD-A-MATCH TACTICS

Board-a-match tactics, in contrast to those in all other varieties of team play, have a great deal in common wtih the match-point tactics discussed in previous chapters. The quantitative element (*how much* better your result is than that at the other table) is completely absent. Thus, the characteristic match-point decisions which assume a large risk to obtain a small advantage—playing games in majors or notrump rather than a minor, playing slams in notrump, light third- and fourth-seat openings, balancing, fierce competition on part-score hands, etc.—are all equally valid at board-a-match. The *differences* spring from one factor: it is no longer possible to win a lot of points on one board; in match points, an occasional "top" can convert a good game into a winning one, but here this important element has vanished.

This shows up clearly in the various types of penalty double decisions. Consider the position in which vulnerable opponents outbid you in a part-score battle when it is "your" hand. At match points, you tend to double whether or not you expect to defeat the contract. The odds are favorable: if they make, you have lost little, since you would be under average anyway, while if you score 200 you get a top. The odds are different for board-a-match; the magnificent 200 number is worth less, and the result if the opponents make their contract undoubled is less likely to be "under average" (you expect your teammates, in whom you have a modicum of confidence, to bid as well as your opponents). Thus, you double only when you have a solid expectation of setting the contract.

Should you double an enemy sacrifice, or bid on to five of your suit? Here, too, there are no longer any considerations of possible tops or bottoms. You expect your teammates to take the same sacrifice, so your decision is clear-cut: if you expect to win eleven tricks more often than not, you bid on; otherwise, you double. Should you double an enemy overcall, or try for your own game? Now that you cannot score a top for a large set, the odds have changed: make only clear-cut doubles; when in doubt, go after your own contract. Should you make a lead-directing double of a slam? If the lead is *likely* to defeat the contract, then yes; if the lead just *possibly* might defeat the contract, then no.

In general, all sorts of "fancy" bids (psychic openings, skinny preempts, wild leaps to game, etc.) should be avoided. Even at match points such tactics are questionable, but they will at least pay off with a top when they work. Toward the end of a pair contest you may decide that a few extraordinarily good results will give you a chance to win; then, it makes sense to "shoot" with daring, unsound bids. But not at board-a-match—here you must sit patiently and grind out your wins and halves. A magnificent result is no better than a normally good one.

The difference in tactics is most marked when you are playing against a pair which you consider inferior. At match points, you tend to be a little more daring in the bidding than usual, trying to build up your score with a top or two while you have the chance. At board-a-match, you should tend to be more *stodgy* than usual; you could ask nothing more than to play the same contract reached at the other table. Then you will win the board whenever your team's declarer or either of your team's defenders plays better than his counterpart—and this means at least three times out of four.

Of course, there is the dark side of the picture—you may be playing against a team *superior* to yours (if such a team could possibly exist). Now you will probably lose any board in which the contract is the same at both tables. So, the odds are all in your favor if you shoot for the moon.

IMP TACTICS

For years, the major United States team-of-four championships (as well as World's Championships) have been scored by International Match Points—IMP's for short. However, there are many players who do not seem to realize the full implications of IMP scoring—how they must alter their normal style. Most of these are tournament regulars who behave as if they were still playing match-point pairs. The games have something in common but there are major differences. Actually, proper play at IMP's lies about halfway between rubber-bridge and match-point styles.

At IMP scoring, any total-point difference between the results at the two tables, any *swing*, is converted into imps on the basis of the following table:

DIFFERENCE IN POINTS	IMP'S	DIFFERENCE IN POINTS	IMP'S
20–40	1	750–890	13
50–80	2	900–1090	14
90–120	3	1100–1290	15
130–160	4	1300–1490	16
170–210	5	1500–1740	17
220–260	6	1750–1990	18
270–310	7	2000–2240	19
320–360	8	2250–2490	20
370–420	9	2500–2990	21
430–490	10	3000–3490	22
500–590	11	3500–3990	23
600–740	12	4000 and up	24

For example, suppose that you bid two hearts and make your contract for +110; at the other table, the opponents bid your cards to *three* hearts and go down one—your teammates are +50. Your team gains a swing of 160 total points, which is converted into 4 imps. Similarly, suppose that your opponents bid four spades and make it—you are −620; your teammates stop at *three* spades when they replay the board, and score +170. Your team loses a swing of 450 total points, or 10 imps.

THE ODDS

Let us calculate the basic odds on bidding games and slams. Bidding a close nonvulnerable game can gain a swing of 250 points—6 imps. If you go down, you may lose a swing of 190 points—5 imps. So the odds are only 6 to 5 in your favor, without allowing for the bad-splitting hand on which you get doubled in game. Really, it is about even money.

Vulnerable games, though, gain 10 imps and lose only 6. Here the odds are much more favorable. So, bid any *vul-*

nerable game that you can sniff faintly; but bid a *nonvulnerable* game only with solid expectation of making it.

For example, suppose you hold:

♠ K 8 4   ♡ A 10 2   ◇ K 7 3   ♣ Q J 10 5

After two passes, you open one club; partner jumps to two notrump. Push on to three notrump if vulnerable, but pass if you are not.

Small slams are even-money bets at imps—you stand to gain or lose the same amount. However, tend to assume that any touch-and-go slam will *not* be bid at the other table. That's a fact of life. Thus, if you are comfortably ahead in the match, or playing a team you rate to beat easily, hold back; but if you are the underdog, play for the swing and bid. Actually, the best chance a weak team has to beat a stronger one is to bounce into slam whenever there seems to be a possibility of making.

Grand slams appear to have odds against them of only 15 to 11 nonvulnerable, or 17 to 13 vulnerable. These are not nearly so prohibitive as the 2 to 1 total-point odds—IMP scoring always reduces the big swing compared to the little one. But there is a hidden factor: at the other table, your opponents may not bid even a small slam. Then, going down in a grand slam vulnerable costs you 26 imps—the 13 you lose, plus the 13 you could have won; and making your grand slam gains only 4 imps extra. Perhaps you think it is next to impossible for the enemy to miss a small slam when you are thinking of a grand slam, but—believe me—it has happened many, many times. *You* no doubt bid most of your slams, but the opponents you play in United States tournaments bid very few. So avoid grand slams unless you can count 13 tricks.

How does all this compare to match-point duplicate? There, it probably pays to bid any game with a 45 percent chance. (You never get a tremendous score for staying out of a close game even when it should go down, for the defense is too often poor; and, after all, you are trying to get a big score and *win* the tournament.) This means that a duplicate buff playing at IMP scoring should be *less* willing than usual to bid a nonvulnerable game but *more* ready to bid a vulnerable game.

Slam bidding is much the same at IMP's as at pairs, but

you are a little readier to bid a doubtful small slam at pairs—since you are more likely to need points urgently. In pairs, as at IMP's, you steer clear of doubtful grand slams, for a small slam bid and made is usually a good score.

1- AND 2-IMP SWINGS

One major difference between IMP's and pair scoring is in the relative insignificance of the extra points for notrump or major suits. You ignore tiny differentials at IMP's, keeping your eye on the main chance—making your contract. Suppose you hold:

♠ Q 4   ♡ Q 8 7 2   ◊ J 2   ♣ A 10 8 7 3

Partner opens one club, you respond one heart, partner rebids one notrump. At match points, you might pass, hoping to make 120; at IMP's, you bid two clubs. This must be safer and you simply do not care whether you score 90 or 110 or 120 or 150.

Now suppose you have the same hand when partner opens one spade. You bid one notrump; partner rebids two clubs. At match points it is surely right to give a false preference to two spades; at IMP's it is surely better to raise clubs. Plus 110 and plus 140 are, in effect, the same at IMP's, and you look for the safest, not the largest, plus.

Obviously, this applies even more forcibly to game and slam contracts. You are perfectly willing to play in a minor suit if it is safer; you never strain to play notrump or major suit contracts simply for the few extra points. Of course, whatever the scoring, it is hard to make five clubs and five diamonds, so these are not common contracts. However, they should be played at IMP's much more often than at match-point pairs.

The answer is: Never even consider swings of 1 or 2 imps. The tiny swings almost always even out over a long match. And if your team goes out to win all the 1-imp and 2-imp swings, I am willing to bet that you will lose the match.

COMPETING FOR PART SCORES

In many respects the fierce competition over part-score hands which characterizes match-point pairs should be carried over into IMP's. That is, you must do a lot of balancing; or, if you prefer, you must get into the auction early and very "lightly." One way or the other, you must *not* let the enemy buy a lot of contracts peacefully at the two-level. The difference between two hearts, making two, and three hearts, down one, may be 5 imps, and a few swings like this can cost you a match.

Now, duplicate-oriented players usually do compete or balance at the two-level when playing IMP's. Where they tend to go wrong is in competing up at the three-level. Here there *is* a big difference between the two games. This is a common dilemma in pairs:

SOUTH	WEST	NORTH	EAST
1 ♠	Pass	2 ♠	Double
Pass	3 ♡	Pass	Pass
?			

You, South, hold:

♠ A Q 8 6 4 ♡ A 8 5 ◇ K 10 4 ♣ J 8

If the cards lie favorably for your side, you might well make three spades; then, you cannot get a good result defending. Likewise, if the lie is unfavorable, the opponents might make three hearts; then, you might do better to go down at three spades. So at match points, you should consider bidding.

At IMP's, though, you should certainly pass. Whether you are plus 140 or plus 100 is a matter of 1 imp; the same is true of minus 100 or minus 140. However, if both three hearts and three spades go down—not at all unlikely—the swing can be 5 imps. If your distribution were unbalanced, so that both contracts might make, then 6 imps might be gained by bidding. But with a flat hand you should expect that only one contract or the other can be made, according to whose finesses work. You cannot lose much by passing, only by bidding.

The key is to think about plus scores on part-score hands —not how big a plus or how small a minus. If I can be plus on three-quarters of the small hands, I will undertake to win almost any match.

Let me illustrate these two different competitive situations with hands from the 1962 World's Championship, played by the United States vs. Argentina. (These are good matches to study for IMP philosophy because of the fundamental differences in approach. Most of the Argentine players are oriented to rubber bridge, while many of our players are oriented to match points.)

NORTH

♠ 7 6 4
♡ K 4 3 2
◇ K 10 5
♣ 9 5 4

WEST

♠ Q 10 9 2
♡ Q 10 7 5
◇ 7 3
♣ A Q 2

EAST

♠ A K J 8 5
♡ 9 6
◇ J 8 4
♣ 8 6 3

SOUTH

♠ 3
♡ A J 8
◇ A Q 9 6 2
♣ K J 10 7

The bidding:

WEST	NORTH	EAST	SOUTH
Pass	Pass	Pass	1 ◇
Double	1 ♡	1 ♠	2 ♡
Pass	Pass	Pass	

There are a number of points of interest in this auction, but I want to concentrate on the Argentine East's final pass. This was (poor) rubber-bridge thinking: "We are both passed hands; the opponents haven't bid game; let sleeping dogs lie." It cost 6 imps, for two hearts made, and the United States made a spade partial at the other table.

```
                     NORTH
                     ♠ 8
                     ♡ 4 3
                     ◇ J 10 8 7 5 2
                     ♣ K 9 8 6

     WEST                          EAST
     ♠ Q J 10 3                    ♠ A 7 6 2
     ♡ A 7 6 5 2                   ♡ Q 9
     ◇ 9 3                         ◇ A K Q 4
     ♣ 10 7                        ♣ 5 4 2

                     SOUTH
                     ♠ K 9 5 4
                     ♡ K J 10 8
                     ◇ 6
                     ♣ A Q J 3
```

The bidding:

SOUTH	WEST	NORTH	EAST
1 ♣	Pass	1 ◇	Pass
1 ♡	Pass	2 ♣	2 ♠
Double	Pass	3 ♣	Pass
Pass	3 ♠	Pass	Pass
4 ♣	Pass	Pass	Pass

Here again the United States was North-South, and here again, we bought the contract at both tables. But now we went down at both, and lost 7 imps.

South's final bid looks to me like match-point thinking: "Partner has long clubs and short spades, so I should have a good play for four clubs; we can beat three spades but not for so good a score." The moral is to fight your opponents up to the three-level and then to play for *any* plus score.

SACRIFICE BIDDING

One area of difference between the match-point and the IMP approach is in sacrificing against game contracts.

Sacrificing can be very rewarding at match points—it is a triumph to lose 300 rather than 420, or 500 rather than 620. At IMP's, though, for the swing of 120 points you earn 3 imps. And this is not a very good return on your investment—that is, for your gamble that the opponents could make their game. True, you are spared the worry of going down too much (losing 700 to save 620, for example, costs only 2 imps). But if you take a phantom sacrifice of 500 points against an unmakable game, you lose 12 imps. So the odds are not nearly so good as at duplicate.

The other side of this picture is that you are much more prone at IMP's than you are at duplicate to double an enemy sacrifice, rather than to push on to five of a major. In a pair game you are reluctant to accept 500 points in exchange for a vulnerable game—it can be almost a zero. Playing IMP's, though, you double a sacrifice bid unless you are a cinch for eleven tricks; the odds are greatly against bidding on.

Of course, I am talking about strictly "match-point"-type sacrifices. In any game it pays to go for 100, or for 300 against a vulnerable game. At any scoring it pays to bid on to five of a major on the chance that you will make it, when you feel that you may not beat the opponents by more than a trick. I do not say "Never sacrifice" or "Always double a sacrifice"; merely remember that the odds are quite different from those at match points, so your normal tendencies must be different also.

Actually, one type of sacrifice is popular among experienced IMP competitors—this is a *premature* sacrifice made in the hope of stampeding the opponents to the five-level. Thus, it aims at a 12-imp, not a 3-imp, profit.

For example, in a recent tournament, I held:

♠ K 6   ♡ A J 7 4   ◇ Q 7 2   ♣ 8 5 4 2

My partner, nonvulnerable against vulnerable, opened three hearts; my right-hand opponent bid three spades; and I jumped to five hearts. Sure enough, my left-hand opponent had a good hand with a spade fit and had to bid five spades—down one.

Another time when a sacrifice aims at a large number of imps is when you save against a slam. Down six doubled,

1100, can gain 8 imps if your partners make 1430. Here is an example (West dealer, East-West vulnerable):

NORTH
♠ K 9 6 5 2
♡ 5
◇ Q 8 5 2
♣ Q 8 4

WEST
♠ A 10 8 4
♡ A Q J 9 7 2
◇ A
♣ 7 6

EAST
♠ Q J
♡ K 10 6 3
◇ K
♣ A K J 9 5 3

SOUTH
♠ 7 3
♡ 8 4
◇ J 10 9 7 6 4 3
♣ 10 2

WEST	NORTH	EAST	SOUTH
1 ♡	2 ♡	Double	7 ◇
Pass	Pass	Double	All pass

North's two-heart bid was, of course, a Michaels Cue-Bid, and South took desperate action fearing a grand slam. Actually, he was right in a way—East-West could make seven clubs, seven hearts or seven notrump, and seven diamonds doubled was down six for 1100 on fine defense. This could gain 15 imps if a grand slam was bid at the other table, or 8 imps otherwise.

What happened? Only *game* was bid by the other East-West pair, so the sacrifice lost 12 imps. You see what I mean about American slam bidding? This is the principal hazard in sacrificing aganst vulnerable slams. It is hard to go for too much if your teammates bid the slam. But since they probably will not, perhaps you should hope to defeat the contract rather than save against it, unless (1) your teammates are unusually aggressive slam bidders, or (2) there seems to be no chance at all of defeating the opposing slam.

PENALTY DOUBLES

In almost all doubling situations at IMP's, the odds favor the coward, not the hero. Consider the position in which vulnerable opponents have crept up to four spades on a shaky auction. You can see that they are running into bad breaks and probably will go down, perhaps even two tricks. Then a double stands to gain 300 points for a two-trick set or to lose 170 should the contract make; but the imp odds are only 7 to 5. And if the opponents' contract is a silly one, your partners probably have stopped at a part score: then a double stands to gain only an imp or two, for you would have a handsome swing in your favor anyway.

This, actually, is quite similar to match-point thinking: Why double the opponents if they have overbid, when you are getting most of the points anyway? And maybe they have not overbid; and maybe your double will allow them to make a contract which otherwise would go down—this is particularly disastrous at IMP's.

An entirely different situation is the one in which you are debating whether to double an enemy overcall or to bid your own game contract. At match points the critical consideration is the vulnerability: can you score in penalties more than the value of your game? For example, suppose you hold:

♠ 7 2　♡ A Q 8　◇ K 9 8 3　♣ K 7 5 4

Partner opens one spade, right-hand opponent overcalls two diamonds. In a pair game you would certainly double if nonvulnerable against vulnerable—a two-trick set seems sure if partner stands the double. You would be reluctant to double on equal vulnerability, for fear that a two-trick set would not equal the score for the game which your side could probably make.

At IMP's, in contrast, you should double at all but the most unfavorable vulnerability. If you lose 100 or 120 points (300 against 420, or 500 against 600), that is only 3 imps. But on the one deal in three when your cards will not produce game, you will win from 8 to 12 imps. So you will gain heavily in the long run, assuming that your own contract is merely *likely*, not certain.

However, suppose you hold:

♠ Q J 8   ♡ K 7 2   ◇ K J 6 4   ♣ A 10 4

With neither side vulnerable, partner opens one spade and right-hand opponent overcalls two diamonds. At match points you might double, hoping to collect 500 (when all you could make was 430 or 460). But at IMP's this swing is worth only 1 or 2 imps; and if you score 300 (against 430 or 460 at the other table) you lose 4 imps. So you will lose in the long run by doubling. Suppose this situation comes up three times in an evening. On each occasion you double the enemy when you have a laydown game yourself, and twice you beat them 500, once 300. At match points you would have two-thirds of the points, a winning percentage. At IMP's you would be minus.

The key question at IMP's, then, is *whether or not your game is sure*. With the first example, you can feel only that game is probable—so you are anxious to play for penalties. Holding the second example, you can hardly imagine a hand that partner can have which will not produce ten or eleven tricks at notrump—so you are reluctant to double. In short, at IMP's, go for the *surest*, not the *greatest*, sizable plus score.

One big difference between the proper match-point and IMP approaches is in doubling enemy part scores on competitive auctions. If you have bid up to three hearts in a pair game and vulnerable opponents contest with three spades, you are likely to double any time you feel sure that your contract would make—you must try to get 200 instead of 100. Obviously, this is suicidal at IMP's. If you score 100 when 140 is made at the other table, you lose 1 imp, and 200 would gain only 2 imps. For this 3-imp pickup, you are risking a loss of 12 imps when the doubled contract is made (and your teammates play it undoubled). At match points, you would gain considerably by doubling such contracts even if one in three is made against you; at IMP scoring you would be a big loser.

Speculative lead-directing doubles (i.e., calling for a lead which does not ensure a set but merely increases your chances) are slightly better bets at IMP's than they are at match points (but not nearly so good at IMP's as at rubber bridge). For example, suppose that you double a non-vulnerable three-notrump contract to get a favorable lead. At match points you are gambling a top against a bottom instead of settling for slightly below average: the odds are little better than even money. To figure the odds at IMP's, assume that the game is bid and made at the other table. If you beat the contract, you gain 500, while if it makes, you lose 150; these total-point odds become 11 imps to 4. The chance of overtricks reduces this to about 2 to 1 in your favor. That is, you will break even if the lead you direct beats one game in three.

The odds become most attractive when it is a slam which you are doubling. Superficially, this does not seem to be so. If you double a nonvulnerable six-spade contract you gain 1080 (15 imps) when you beat it, while you lose 230 (6 imps) if you do not. But this assumes that the contract is the same at the other table, and this is an unwarranted assumption in the case of a close slam (as distinct from a touch-and-go game which probably will be bid). If only game is reached at the other table, your loss from doubling a makable slam is 1 imp; and when your double was necessary to defeat the slam, your gain is 22 imps. (You gain 11 instead of losing 11.) At odds of 22 to 1, it is hard to go wrong.

GENERAL TACTICS

I have covered quite a few specific situations in which the differences between IMP's and match-point scoring create a difference in approach: stretching for vulnerable games, ignoring tiny swings, competing or selling out on part-score hands, sacrificing, doubling. There is another area of difference, though, caused not so much by the scoring as by the objectives of the two games.

At match points, you are trying to beat some huge (and it will be bigger next year) number of competing pairs. At IMP's, you are trying to beat one team (at a time). And, in a pair contest, the huge field usually means that a great number of poor and inexperienced players are your direct or indirect opponents. But in an IMP team game you are not likely to meet any really bad opponents. What this means is that it is probably the winning style at match points to try to beat par, to try for unusually good results; in contrast, at IMP scoring this is not the winning style (unless you are far behind or a decided underdog).

Par bridge—i.e., taking everything which is yours without trying to steal what belongs to the enemy—will win almost any IMP match. Of course, you and your teammates are bound to make a few errors, but if you play a steady game and make fewer mistakes than the opponents, you will win. A 51 percent game is good enough. At match points, a 51 percent game is a disaster; even 60 percent games will not win tournaments. You must take more chances (and this means make more bad bids) to win a pair game.

One illustration of this is in preemptive bidding. Playing match points, I would probably open this hand:

♠ 6   ♡ K Q 10 8 6 4   ◇ A J 10 6 3   ♣ 2

with four hearts, first hand, neither side vulnerable. At IMP's, I would want better heart spots to protect me against disaster, and I would worry more about the possibility that we might belong in diamonds. Thus, I would open one heart. At IMP's I would not be "out stealing"; I would go slow, to find out what we can actually make.

Another illustration is in balancing in risky positions, that is, when the opponents have not found a fit. Suppose that the auction goes as follows:

WEST	NORTH	EAST	SOUTH
1 NT	Pass	Pass	?

With neither side vulnerable, I hold, sitting South:

♠ K 10 8 4 3   ♡ 5   ◇ A 10 6 5   ♣ Q 7 4

At match points I would bid two spades. If I pass, I am settling for a normal under-average score, and I would rather try to beat par with an unsound overcall. At IMP's, I would pass, accepting the fact that it is "wrong" to overcall. The risk of a disastrous result is one I do not have to take when I am trying to beat one team instead of two hundred pairs.

In the bridge world there are quite a few famous players whose great strength is their tactical bidding. (A "tactical" bid is a bad bid which gets a good result.) These experts do very well at match points, winning far more than their share of tournaments, killing the weak fields. But they do poorly in team games.

So, save your bad bids for match points. When you play IMP's, try a cautious, cowardly style; leave the heroics to your opponents. Then, at the end of the match you can compliment them on some brilliant bid, while they are congratulating you for winning.

IX. SYSTEMS, CONVENTIONS AND TREATMENTS

Most of this chapter will be devoted to the description of the systems, conventions, gadgets and bizarre bidding methods that you will encounter in the world of duplicate bridge. There is no reason on earth for you to use more than a few of them yourself (if you try to use them all, you will exasperate your partners and infuriate your opponents). However, it is to your advantage to *learn* them all.

Partly, this is in order to appear sophisticated; you lose face when you have to inquire about the meaning of some cryptic notation on the enemy convention card. Your main objective, of course, is to be sufficiently aware of your opponents' methods to take a shrewd guess as to the nature of their hands, and to be able to exploit the weakness of their gadgets. Therefore, *my* purpose is not to teach you how to use these various devices; I will try to show you what they are, and how to defend against them.

First, let us examine what it is that the opponents must announce to you, and you to them. In theory, no player is allowed to know more about the meaning of his partner's bid than do the opponents. In practice, though, every established parnership has understandings of which their opponents are unaware. (Player A often opens the bidding in third seat with a 9- or 10-point hand; Player B is likely to open with "three" on hands that sensible people open with "one"; Player C feels free to open "one spade" with a four-card suit headed by the ten. Their regular partners can expect and allow for these foibles; their opponents cannot.) These are matters of "partnership style" and, since it is simply impossible to list or describe such nebulous tendencies, no attempt is usually made to announce them. There are three great areas of partnership agreement that *do* call for announcement on the convention card: I shall call them conventions, treatments and systems.

By a **convention,** I mean a bid which names a suit (or notrump) without any suggestion that *this* is the declaration at which the contract should be played, without any promise of values in the suit bid. A convention is an artificial bid, a sort of code message, which asks partner a question or instructs him to choose a suit, or shows values elsewhere. A familiar example (so familiar, in fact, that you do not have to announce it—you are assumed to be playing it) is the Blackwood convention, in which four notrump says nothing about notrump but, instead, asks a "code" question about aces. The convention of longest standing is the takeout double. The natural sense of "Double" is for penalties; the usage which means, "Bid your best suit, partner" is artificial, conventional. Obviously, this ancient convention need not be announced; in fact, you must tell the opponents if you do *not* use it. But *all* conventional devices other than the two above, all code bids with artificial meanings, must be fully and clearly disclosed to the opponents in advance.

The bids which I classify as **treatments** are all *natural,* rather than *artificial;* that is, they are legitimate offers to play in the suit named. Why must they be announced, then? It is because there are areas in which differing partnership understandings give such widely disparate strength values to the same bids. For instance, suppose that your partner opens with one diamond and your right-hand opponent jumps to two spades. Nearly every partnership * uses this as a natural bid, promising great length in spades. However, the *strength* shown by the bid can be 16 to 19 points (strong jump overcall), or 12 to 15 points (intermediate jump overcall), or 6 to 11 points (preemptive jump overcall). How can you act intelligently without knowing what the enemy bid promises? So, a special place is provided on the convention card to indicate the meaning of the jump overcall. The opening two-bid is treated similarly (about half of your opponents will open two hearts with a hand too *strong* for a one-heart bid, the other half with a hand too *weak*—their cards are marked accordingly).

---

* There is one tiny group, though, who promise length in *clubs* with this bid—*their* jump overcall is what I call a "convention" rather than a "treatment."

The general principle is that the opponents must be informed of the strength promised by your bids, within vague limits (say, whether the bid is forcing, or invitational or preemptive). In areas like the ones above, in which there is no general agreement about strength, the convention card has special listings in which you *must* indicate what your partnership understanding is. There are other areas in which there *is* a standard practice; for example, eight players out of ten use a jump raise (one diamond–three diamonds) as a forcing bid. If you make no announcement, it is assumed that your agreement is the standard one; if you have an unusual understanding (for example, that the jump raise is *preemptive*, or merely *invitational*), you must write it down on your card. Note that this applies only to a *major* divergence from standard practice. The opponents need not be burdened with tiny differences (whether you play a raise of one spade to two spades as 6 to 9, or 7 to 10 points); these are properly considered matters of "style."

A **system** is a complex group of treatments and conventions gathered together as a unit to complement one another. Partnerships which use a system often attempt to give narrower-than-normal definitions of meaning to their bids. Some of their ordinary-sounding sequences will have unusual inferences attached. And all of the partnerships which use one system will have in common certain features of style and tactics. Therefore, it is customary to make an announcement on the convention card (right on top, where it says "General Approach") if a system is being used. However, this in no way affects the obligation to announce, separately, the conventions and treatments employed.

SYSTEMS

Suppose that you and I decide to play regularly together, and to devise our own language of bidding. The cornerstone of our method, we agree, is that when we hold a normal opening bid in a *black* suit we will open one diamond with a minimum, one heart with a maximum; similarly, with *red* suit openings, we will start with one club when light and one spade when heavy. Next, we invent a whole host of conventions to enable us to handle the second round of bidding; we round off our system with a batch of special treatments forced upon us by our artificial conventions. We flex our muscles in a few home games—we do well, since *we* understand what we are doing, while the opponents have scarcely any idea of what our bids mean. All that remains is to name our system (we call it the "Black Diamond"), and to try it out in a club duplicate or tournament.

Alas, the director takes one look at our convention card, with "Black Diamond" flying jauntily at its masthead and a thick underbrush of gimmicks and gadgets lurking beneath—and he tells us that we cannot use our system. He is quite right, too. The A.C.B.L. is not concerned with the name which we gave our methods—it does not license or forbid whole systems. But if our system involves a set of complicated and unusual conventions which the opponents cannot possibly understand thoroughly after a few seconds' study, then our *conventions* (not our system) will, and should, be barred. Otherwise, we would have an unfair advantage over everyone else.

Thus, no duplicate player need worry about having to cope suddenly with someone's home-made system. Even the famous Italian systems are forbidden in pair contests—their conventions are too complex. (In major team championships, where one plays long matches against a single opponent, these rules are relaxed.) In the United States, there are only three systems which are played by a substantial number of duplicate enthusiasts: Roth-Stone, Kaplan-Sheinwold and the Schenken Club.

If you wish to learn how to play these systems yourself, buy the books which describe them (*Bridge Is a Partnership Game,* by Alvin Roth; *The Kaplan-Sheinwold System of Winning Bridge,* by Edgar Kaplan and Alfred Sheinwold; *Better Bridge in Fifteen Minutes,* by Howard Schenken). What I set forth below is, in general, what you need to know in order to contend with the systems as an opponent.

ROTH-STONE SYSTEM

The distinguishing feature of Roth-Stone is not its impressive array of gadgets, even though many of the unusual treatments and conventions currently in play were introduced through this system. What makes Roth-Stone markedly different from Standard American is its tempo. Most bids in the early auction are extremely conservative. First- and second-hand opening bids require solid high-card values—perhaps one out of every four Standard openings is passed. Opener's rebids seem incredibly timid (he has, you see, already shown an excellent hand by opening at all). Responder needs virtually the values for game to go to the two-level with his first bid, or to bid freely (even at the one-level) over an enemy overcall. And responder's rebids follows the same pattern. For example, consider this sequence:

OPENER	RESPONDER
1 ♠	2 ◇
2 ♠	3 ◇

In Standard bidding, this indicates two limited hands which will have to be lucky to scramble home with the nine tricks to make a part score. In Roth-Stone, however, this could easily be the start of a *slam* auction. Opener's hand is *unlimited*, since partner's two-over-one response guarantees a further bid. Responder's rebid is not really a signoff, since his first action promised such great strength; and he knows that partner will not feel like passing, for the Roth-Stone opening bid is never a scratchy minimum. Obviously, a different language is being spoken—do you see what I mean about tempo?

Defensive bidding is similar. The takeout double shows a powerful hand, and doubler will tend to rebid over partner's conservative response. The direct overcall is sound, based, usually, on the values for an opening bid. Does all this make you wonder how Roth-Stone players ever get into the auction when all they can make is a part score? The system has two answers to this problem.

The first is a strong tendency toward "balancing" action. To protect against their own mountainous passes in first and second seat, Roth-Stoners will open very skinny hands in third or fourth position. On auctions in which *your* side makes the opening bid, they may leave the first few rounds of bidding to you. But when you pass out at the two-level, they will come galloping in with reopening doubles or overcalls, even after bidding sequences which do not seem to call for balancing.

The other feature of Roth-Stone which spices up the basically stodgy style is a broad spectrum of preemptive bids. The same players who lumber cautiously to their final contract when they hold powerful hands will leap about like trapeze artists when their distribution is exciting and their point count low. The general Roth-Stone approach can be summed up like this: Keep the auction low, saving all your bidding room on big hands; do your jumping on shapely, weak hands, so as to impede the opponents; with in-between hands, wait and listen.

ROTH-STONE CONVENTIONS AND TREATMENTS

First- or second-seat opening bids in a *major* suit guarantee five cards or more. Since the two-over-one response is so powerful, one notrump is the most common response to a major opening—this is played as a *force* (see p. 144). The single raise, from one to two in the major, is highly constructive (at least 10 points, usually more; with less strength, responder first bids one notrump, then shows his support); it is virtually forcing, since a Roth-Stone opening plus a constructive raise adds up to game, or close to it. The *jump* raise, therefore, is not merely a force; it carries strong slam implications. In third or fourth position, the opening bid may be in a four-card major suit, but only when opener has a subminimum hand and intends to pass partner's response. With a sound minimum, he opens and rebids normally; he may, after all, make game opposite a Roth-Stone pass.

Minor-suit openings are often made on three-card suits. This hand:

♠ K J 7 4   ♡ A Q J 3   ◇ 8 6 4   ♣ K 6

is opened *one diamond* in any position. Responses, with four-card suits, are "up the line"; that is, the cheaper suit is bid first without regard to quality. If opener raises the response, he guarantees four-card support and solid values. The response of one notrump to a minor opening is not forcing, but is mildly constructive (particularly to one club). On occasional awkward hands, the response may be made in a three-card suit (most often one diamond to one club, but sometimes a major response). With this sequence:

OPENER	RESPONDER
1 ◇	1 ♡
2 ♡	2 NT

opener has shown a sound opening bid with four hearts (quite possibly only three diamonds). Responder has indicated an interest in game, but most likely a *three*-card heart suit.

Jump-shift responses to any first- or second-hand opening bids are preemptive. Thus, a response of one spade followed by a rebid of two spades promises a decent hand; responder's *jump* rebid of his first suit is forcing and unlimited—this jump could be in place of the *strong* jump shift. Many other preemptive treatments and conventions are employed. Weak two-bids fit in well with the system; they may be made on hands that you or I would consider strong enough for a one-bid. Michaels Cue-Bids complement the sound takeout double; weak jump overcalls do the same for the solid *simple* overcall. The Roth-Stone style, in using any of the preemptive devices above, is for the player who has made the weak bid to remain silent thereafter, for the *partner* to do any sacrifice bidding that is called for.

The system uses both negative and responsive doubles. This helps compensate for a peculiar Roth-Stone phobia—the reluctance to make a free bid.

Roth-Stone players open psychics in first or second position. The suit itself will be honest, and the psycher's strength will be from 2 to 6 points.

COUNTERMEASURES TO ROTH-STONE

It often pays to open light and respond aggressively when playing against Roth-Stoners. They tend to rely on the sound of *your* bidding, so if you sound strong enough, you may steal hands from them. Remember, though, that if you subside at the two-level they will balance; so with distributional values, keep going up to three (see Preemptive Reraise, p. 141). In contrast, with powerful *defensive* values you may be well advised to pass out at the two-level rather than make a sketchy try for game; your opponents may reopen and give you a juicy penalty. When your side has the early auction all to itself, as it often will against Roth-Stoners, you have these extra tactical opportunities, but there is a danger too—be sure that you do not credit your partner with extra strength merely because the enemy is silent.

When your opponents *do* enter the auction early, treat their bidding with respect. Be wary of speculative penalty doubles—except in its preemptive or balancing bidding, the cautious Roth-Stone approach will give you few opportunities to get rich from sets. If your left-hand opponent bids one spade and the response, on your right, is two clubs, take advantage of their solid style and stay out of the auction. You are heavily outgunned, and competition will only help *them*. In general, be conservative in all your defensive bidding (it is all right to overcall or double for takeout or, rarely, balance, but be sure not to get up very high). Remember, Roth-Stoners like to have a little extra strength in reserve.

KAPLAN-SHEINWOLD SYSTEM

Kaplan-Sheinwold has a number of conventions and treatments in common with Roth-Stone, but its approach to bidding is entirely different. The cornerstone of the system is the weak one-notrump opening. All balanced hands of 12 to 14 points are opened (if at all) with one notrump. Thus, a suit opening bid implies either an unbalanced or a strong hand.

Major-suit opening bids promise five-card or greater length. If this requirement is met, however, a hand is opened upon the slightest excuse (12 high card points, or 2½ quick tricks, or considerable playing strength). These are one-spade openings in K-S:

♠ A Q 10 8 6   ♥ A 7 5 3   ♦ 6 4   ♣ 8 2
♠ A 10 9 8 4 3   ♥ 2   ♦ A 10 9 2   ♣ 7 5

In contrast, minor-suit opening bids are sounder. Neither hand above would be opened if the long suit were clubs.

An opening in a minor will contain 15 points or more if it is a balanced hand; unbalanced hands will usually have 12 or 13 high-card points. Even here, though, lighter hands may be opened if they have great playing power combined with 2½ or 3 quick tricks.

In effect, then, Kaplan-Sheinwold opens many *more* hands than does Standard bidding. And the same tendency is carried over into defensive bidding. The takeout double is employed with 11-, 10- or even 9-point hands; the principal requirement is not high cards but shape—support for all unbid suits. Overcalls promise a more substantial point count. However, the system does not require a pass on any hand with merely *playing* strength—weak jump overcalls are used freely and friskily.

Thus, the style of Kaplan-Sheinwold is exactly the opposite of Roth-Stone's. It is to get into the auction early, and to make a limit bid on the first or second round.

KAPLAN-SHEINWOLD CONVENTIONS AND TREATMENTS

The weak notrump opening is, of course, the most common limit bid. Its range is 12 to 14 points (conceivably 11 points with 3 quick tricks, or 15 points with 1½ quick tricks). Responder places the contract just as in Standard bidding over strong notrumps. Responder will seldom pass with fewer than 5 points, preferring instead to escape to a suit. The Stayman two-club response is occasionally used as a semi-psychic for this purpose.

The system uses Five-Card Majors, but not rigorously. Strong four-card suits may be treated as five-carders, usually when a touching lower-ranking suit is held. The response of one notrump is forcing. The single raise of opener's major is weak. (If opener then tries for game by bidding a new suit, this is likely a singleton.) The jump raise is invitational; a direct response of three notrump is conventional—this is the forcing raise. A two-over-one response in a *minor* suit is strong, and creates many game-forcing positions unless responder rebids his suit; however, a two-heart response to one spade is of standard strength.

The opening bid in a minor is often on a three-card suit, but then always with a strong hand. Responder goes out of his way to answer in a major suit, even bypassing a five-card minor to bid a four-card major. The response of one notrump is very weak. Two clubs in answer to one diamond may be weaker than standard. Minor-suit raises are "inverted": the jump raise is weak, but the single raise is forcing. Opener, with the strong balanced hand, will rebid in notrump or, with four-card support, raise partner's major. With an unbalanced hand, opener will rebid his minor (or, when possible, bid a major at the one-level) when he has minimum strength; he will usually bid a new suit when he holds extra values.

All third- and fourth-hand opening bids are assumed to be sound, and the auctions which follow them are unchanged. Subminimum hands are opened, if at all, with weak notrumps or weak two-bids. Weak two-bids are highly disciplined, and thus rare, in first or second seat (1½ to 2 quick tricks, semisolid six-card suit); for third or fourth hand, the requirements are relaxed.

Psychics are as in Roth-Stone. They are "controlled" by the jump shift, which is strong and is forcing even on a psychic. However, the jump shift becomes preemptive after an intervening overcall or takeout double. In addition, the jump shift is weak when made by a passed hand. (K-S players never pass hands with which they wish to bid that strongly later.)

COUNTERMEASURES TO KAPLAN-SHEINWOLD

When you are playing against a Kaplan-Sheinwold pair, there are a few special auctions to watch out for. This one is very common:

OPENER	YOU	RESPONDER	PARTNER
1 ♡	Pass	1 NT	Pass
2 ♣	Pass	2 ♡	Pass
Pass	?		

This *sounds* like a position in which you should tend to balance, but it is not. Your opponents have *not* found a heart fit—responder has only a doubleton heart, since he did not raise directly. A reopening double here is best played for penalties.

Do not be too eager to make "cheap" overcalls at the

one-level after a minor-suit opening. Remember, your opponent has, more often than not, a powerful balanced hand, a strong notrump. So your bid is far more likely to help the opponents than to help you. Although it seems riskier, the overcall at the two-level after a *major* opening is safer and more likely to be profitable, since major-suit openings may be made on trash.

Finally, be sure that you and partner have discussed your defenses against the weak notrump opening (see p. 124). Your outstanding chance to profit from your opponents' system occurs when the notrump opening is facing a Yarborough. But you must have the mechanism to let you cash in on the enemy misfortune.

SCHENKEN CLUB SYSTEM

The Schenken Club system, or the "Big Club" as it is sometimes called, is a variation on an old theme, one that has long fascinated bridge theoreticians (as in the Vanderbilt Club, the Neapolitan Club, and countless other "club" systems). The central idea is that an artificial opening bid of one club is reserved for any hand very rich in high cards. All *other* opening bids are at once limited by the failure to open one club; thus, the auctions can be developed more accurately.

One of the attractive features of the Schenken system is that most of its auctions are familiar to players used to Standard bidding. Oh, there are a few artificial sequences, particularly following the one-club or two-club openings (two clubs is the opening for a minimum hand containing a long club suit). But most auctions start with one diamond, one heart or one spade, and proceed quite normally.

However, the inferences from the failure to open "one club" create some variations in style or treatment. Opener can bid with sketchier-than-usual values, since his hand is already limited; similarly, opener's strong-sounding rebids —jumps, reverses—can be made freely with *distributional*, rather than high-card, strength. Responder can pass the opening bid or the rebid with moderate values (enough to force him to keep the auction alive in Standard), for he is often in a position to judge immediately that game is impossible. And responder can jump directly to game (one spade, four spades) with *either* the preemptive pattern or a substantial high-card structure; he need not fear missing slam when he is strong, since opener is limited.

The principal advantage of the Schenken system is the ease with which it distinguishes among various levels of strong opening bids. Consider these three hands:

(1)   ♠ K Q J 10 7 6 4   ♡ A Q 4   ◇ 7 4   ♣ 2
(2)   ♠ K Q J 7 6 4   ♡ A Q 4   ◇ A 4   ♣ 7 2
(3)   ♠ A K J 7 6 4   ♡ A K J   ◇ A 4   ♣ 7 2

All three are Standard one-spade openings; with all three, the Standard bidder feels like jumping at his second turn. Yet they vary enormously in strength. In Schenken, these hands present no problem. Example (1) is opened one spade, and a jump rebid in spades describes it perfectly. With (2) and (3), the opening is one club; opener then treats (2) as a minimum, while he shows further enthusiasm for (3).

SCHENKEN CLUB CONVENTIONS AND TREATMENTS

The opening bid of one club is artificial and forcing, promising 17 points or more in high cards (with exceptional playing strength plus a long major suit, this requirement may be lowered slightly). The response of one diamond is negative, showing 0 to 8 points. Any other response is positive (9 points or more) and game forcing. Positive responses are natural, showing long (five-card or strong four-card) suits. Lacking a long suit, responder may bid notrump: one (9 to 11); two (12 or 13); three (14 or 15). Jump responses promise solid suits (but two *diamonds* is merely a *positive*, not a *jump* response). If the one-club opening is overcalled, *double* is conventional, showing a positive response; any other action denies 9 points. Similarly, after a takeout double, *redouble* is the positive response.

The one-club opener rebids naturally. After a negative response, a nonjump rebid may be passed; a jump rebid in a suit is forcing for one round, showing, typically, a Standard forcing two-bid. However, after a *positive* response this jump rebid promises merely a solid suit. A rebid of one notrump promises even distribution with 18 to 20 points (the *opening bid* of one notrump shows 15 to 17 points); a rebid of two notrump promises 21 or 22 points (the *opening bid* of two notrump is "unusual" showing a minor two-suiter). Stronger balanced hands are opened *two diamonds* (see below). Over all notrump responses to one club, and over all notrump rebids by the one club opener, partner may use Stayman by bidding the minimum number of clubs necessary.

Opening bids of one diamond, one heart or one spade are natural, but limited to a maximum of 16 points. Four-card major suits are opened freely, but the suit should be headed by a high honor. Responder's raise is mildly constructive (8 to 11 points), since he need not bid at all; actually any response, even one notrump, tends to be progressive for this reason. Responder's jump to *two* notrump shows 12 or 13 points and is nonforcing. The opening bid of one diamond is frequently a bid of convenience on a three-card suit (the short *club* is not available). Thus, responder strains a little more to bid over one diamond than he does after a major opening. After any of these openings, if opener's rebid is in *clubs* he is likely to be longer in clubs than in his first suit; therefore, responder is reluctant to give a preference.

The opening bid of two clubs describes a hand of up to 16 points containing a long club suit. The suit itself should be of the length and strength to justify an *overcall* at the two-level. Of these hands:

(4)	♠ A 10 7 3	♡ 6 4	◇ A Q	♣ K 8 6 4 3
(5)	♠ A J 6	♡ 6 4	◇ A Q 4	♣ Q 10 6 4 3
(6)	♠ A J 6 3	♡ 2	◇ K 4	♣ K Q 10 6 4 3

only (6) is a two-club opening. The proper opening with (4) is one spade; with (5) it is one diamond.

In reponse to the two-club opening, bids of two hearts, two spades or three clubs are natural and nonforcing. Two diamonds is forcing and may be artificial, requesting opener to bid a major suit if he has one (as in example (6) above). Two notrump is forcing also, but tends to deny interest in major-suit play.

The opening bid of *three* clubs is not a normal preempt. It promises a long *solid* club suit, possibly in a hand with the values for a minimum opening bid. Partner is invited to try for three notrump.

The two-diamond opening bid is artificial, forcing and very strong. The responses are ace-showing (with no ace, two hearts; with the heart ace, two notrump; with any other ace, its suit; with two aces, a jump), and opener can later find out about specific kings and queens. This opening bid is employed in place of one club when opener has a freak hand and requires specific cards, not general strength, from partner. However, it is also used to describe an enormously powerful balanced hand. Then, opener rebids two notrump (23 or 24 points) or three notrump (25 or 26 points).

Opening bids of two hearts and two spades are normal weak two-bids.

COUNTERMEASURES TO SCHENKEN CLUB

When your right-hand opponent opens with the Big Club bid, bear two factors in mind: no matter how good your hand is, your opponent's is probably better, so it is dangerous to bid; your opponent has not yet bid his real suit, and may be completely unable to describe his hand if the auction gets up high very fast, so it can be rewarding to bid. What this means is that your high cards should not tempt you to bid if you have tame distribution; but your wild distribution should get you into the auction even if you have very few points. Any action should show playing strength, not high cards—two spades, for example, should show better distribution than *one* spade, but denies enough winners to bid *three* spades. You might use "double" for a major two-suiter, "one notrump" for a minor two-suiter. (A more sophisticated method of defending with two-suiters over the Big Club has been suggested by Alan Truscott. Any nonjump overcall shows a specific two-suiter—the suit bid and the next-higher-ranking one; a double shows clubs and hearts; one notrump shows diamonds and spades. With *one*-suiters, jump-overcall. I recommend this defense to partnerships with good memories.) Everything said above applies even more forcibly when the opening is two diamonds. Here, it may be crucial to disrupt the enemy auction.

Against the other opening bids, use your normal style

of defensive bidding. You can afford to be slightly aggressive, resolving any doubt in favor of action, since the opening is limited. Beware of some of the systemic features already detailed. Do not be eager to balance when a one-bid is passed out; bid only if you would have *directly* over the opening. Do not assume that responder is weak if he jumps directly to game in opener's major; responder may have 14 high-card points. Remember to be a little suspicious of the one-diamond opening bid. On this enemy auction:

OPENER	RESPONDER
1 ♢	1 ♡
1 NT	3 NT

opener is just as likely to have a *club* suit as a diamond suit, so choose your opening lead accordingly.

CONVENTIONS

The A.C.B.L. has stern views as to which conventions will be permitted in tournament play. It has a list of the best-known devices, with which all players are presumed to be familiar; these must be allowed. It has a secondary list of more specialized gadgets which *may* be allowed at the option of the local powers-that-be. There is even a third list of recondite conventions to be allowed only in long team matches. And all others are barred. You cannot roll your own.

Before presenting my descriptions of the conventions you will encounter most often (all of them fall into one of the first two categories above), let me discuss how you should *defend* against artificial bids in general. My suggestion is that you and your partner agree on these three principles:

1. Over *strong* artificial enemy bids (like Gerber, ace-showing responses and Stayman), your double is for penalties, largely lead-directing, showing values in the suit you double.

2. Over what may be *weak* artificial bids (typically, takeout conventions such as Michaels Cue-Bids and the unusual notrump, used over your openings), your double

is strictly strength-showing, saying nothing in particular about the suit you double.

3. When the artificial bid promises length in some *other* specific suit (as in transfer bids, for instance), your bid of that promised suit, the "real" enemy suit, is for takeout, showing values elsewhere.

For example, suppose that the auction goes:

OPENER	YOU	RESPONDER	PARTNER
1 NT	Pass	2 ♣	Double

What does partner's double mean? Look at the opponents' convention card. If the two-club response is natural, showing clubs, partner's action is a normal takeout double. If responder's bid is Stayman, a strong artificial bid, partner is telling you to lead clubs. If the opponents use *two-way* Stayman (2 diamonds strong, 2 clubs weak), then partner has doubled a *weak* artificial bid: he has a lot of high cards, and wants you to compete or to penalize the opponents. If the two-club bid is a transfer bid promising a *diamond* suit, partner's double shows *clubs;* if he had wanted you to take out, he would have bid diamonds—the real enemy suit.

The three principles above represent my recommendations for defense against most of the conventional bids which follow. I have specified a defense only if I feel that, for some reason or other, the general defense should not apply.

STAYMAN AND OTHERS

I am sure that you know what **Stayman** is—the two-club response to one notrump asking for opener to bid a major suit if he has one. What I plan to discuss here are the various modifications, extensions and treatments which you may encounter. The convention is seldom played today in its original form. Few players use the two-notrump rebid to show a maximum notrump; instead, they rebid two diamonds whenever they have no major. Many players no longer show a weak response with long clubs by bidding first two clubs, then three clubs; instead, they jump to three clubs directly when weak, using Stayman first only when strong—and some extend this treatment to diamonds as well. (This should be noted on the convention card—"jump response in clubs [minors] is weak" or some such.)

The difference between **nonforcing** and **forcing Stayman** has to do with this common auction:

OPENER	RESPONDER
1 NT	2 ♣
2 ◊	2 ♡ (or 2 ♠)

In the nonforcing variation, opener is allowed to pass responder's rebid of two in a major. He is not *compelled* to pass; responder would bid two hearts immediately if he had no interest in game, so opener will try for game with maximum values or good fit—but he *may* pass. In the forcing variation, opener may *not* pass—after the Stayman response, opener must keep going until the partnership reaches two notrump or three in a major. Incidentally, be on your toes against opponents who use forcing Stayman. Responder, above, may be trying to stop a heart lead; if he is raised, he will retreat to three notrump.

Carter or **Two-Way Stayman** uses *both* variations. Two diamonds asks for majors and promises the values for game; thus, all sequences which follow it are forcing. Two clubs asks for majors, but is used either to find the right part score or to invite game. Note that two clubs can be bid even when responder has a terrible hand without the slightest interest in game. The earlier example auction is a *signoff* in Carter; *three* of a major after two clubs is the invitational sequence.

Murray Two Diamonds is one of several similar conventions in which the response of two *diamonds* to one notrump forces opener to bid his better major suit, even a three-card suit if necessary. Responder may have two five-card majors himself, and want to find out which one opener prefers. Or, responder may have only one five-card major; if he does not raise (or pass) the suit opener picks, then responder has five cards in the *other* major.

Flint is a convention used over *two*-notrump openings. The response of *three diamonds* is used in order to sign off at three of a major suit. Opener is compelled to rebid three hearts. Now responder will pass if hearts is his suit, or bid three spades and be allowed to play there. Note the difference between Flint and the transfer bids which follow: responder does *not* promise hearts when he bids three diamonds; he may have spades instead; he may even have intended his diamond bid as natural—this is what it means if responder neither passes three hearts nor bids three spades at his second turn.

JACOBY AND TEXAS TRANSFERS

Transfer bids are conventional responses to notrump openings designed to allow opener—who presumably has the strong hand which should be led *up to*, not *through*—to become declarer in responder's long suit. In **Texas Transfer,** the response of *four diamonds* to a one-notrump or two-notrump opening bid forces opener to bid four hearts; the response of *four hearts* forces opener to bid four spades. Presumably, responder is very long not in the suit he bids but in the next-higher-ranking one. In practice, there have been some spectacular and embarrassing mishaps, particularly with the artificial four-heart response (which has a natural sound). This has led to a variation called (so help me!) **South African Texas** in which four *clubs* demands hearts, four *diamonds* demands spades. This is less accident-prone, but gets in the way of the Gerber convention.

Jacoby Transfers operate on the same principle, but are used at the *two-level* over one notrump or at the *three-level* over two notrump. The response of two diamonds to one notrump requests opener to bid two hearts (opener may bid *three* hearts instead, but this is rare). After opener's dutiful rebid, responder may pass two hearts or invite game with three hearts, or leap to four hearts, according to his strength. He may, instead, bid two notrump or three notrump; these are natural bids, but opener is at liberty to correct to hearts, for responder has promised five. Similarly, responder may continue with a new suit over two hearts; this is forcing, and describes a two-suiter—the suit he bids plus hearts. The sequences described are identical in meaning if the response to one notrump is two hearts, but now, of course, responder has promised spades. A direct response of two *spades* is used to suggest a minor-suit slam.

LANDY, RIPSTRA AND ASTRO

Many duplicate players feel the need for a convention which will enable them to compete more effectively after an enemy opening bid of one notrump. The first, and still the most popular, of these is **Landy.** Landy is an artificial bid of *two clubs* over an opposing one-notrump opening (originally only over a *weak* notrump; now, commonly, over any range) used as a sort of takeout double. There is a school which uses Landy as a light takeout of unspecified distributional pattern. The usual expert interpretation, however, is that Landy is a request for the majors. Partner will answer by taking his choice between hearts and spades, bidding a three-card suit if required. He is *allowed* to bid two diamonds or pass two clubs, but only in case of emergency. The Landy bidder promises at least four cards in each major, and often has five in one or both; the more freakish his pattern the less high-card strength he needs.

Ripstra is a variation in which both *two clubs* and *two diamonds* are used as takeout bids requesting a reply in a major. The bidder will select his better (longer, stronger) minor suit for his action. Therefore, while partner will respond much as to Landy, he is better placed to pass the only *semi*artificial takeout. Note this: the Ripstra bidder is very likely to have a singleton or void in the minor suit he does not bid.

Astro uses both *two clubs* and *two diamonds* for takeout, but each bid promises only *one* major, not both. The Astro takeout is made with a two-suited hand (no fewer than nine cards in the two suits); at least one of the suits is a major. Two *diamonds* indicates *spades* plus another unspecified suit; two *clubs* indicates *hearts* plus a minor suit (not spades as well, for then the takeout would be two diamonds). Partner answers by supporting the indicated major if he has three or four cards in it. Failing this, usually he makes the artificial "neutral" response of the next-higher suit (two *diamonds* over two clubs; two *hearts* over two diamonds); then the Astro bidder shows his five-card suit, conceivably by passing the neutral response. Two notrump, bid by either partner at any stage, is forcing and asks for further information.

Partnerships who use any of these three conventions treat the double of one notrump as strictly for penalties.

FISHBEIN, CHEAPER MINOR, WEISS, SMITH

Fishbein is a convention designed to allow the double of an enemy opening three-bid to be for *penalties*, rather than have it be the usual takeout or optional double. Here, the takeout bid is the overcall in the next higher suit (three *diamonds* over three clubs; three *spades* over three hearts). This artificial takeout is forcing; partner must bid his longer unbid suit or raise the takeout. Some players use Fishbein only *directly over* the preemptive opening; others use it in the reopening position as well.

Cheaper Minor is a variation of Fishbein in which the takeout bid is never made in a major suit. It is still three diamonds over three clubs; however, it is four clubs over any other three-bid. Thus, major-suit overcalls are natural and nonforcing.

In **Weiss,** the cheaper minor is the artificial takeout bid employed. However, the double is *not* strictly for penalties. Instead, it shows a relatively balanced hand, rich in high cards, which is more suitable for defense than for attack. Partner should take out if *his* hand is unbalanced; otherwise he will convert this "optional" double into a penalty double by passing.

In **Smith,** the artificial takeout is invariably four clubs; however, in the reopening position overcalls are all natural and double is for takeout.

All of these conventions are commonly adapted for defense against weak two-bids as well.

MICHAELS AND OTHER CUE-BIDS

The **Michaels Cue-Bid** is the overcall in the enemy suit, directly over the opening bid, used as a distributional takeout—a light takeout double. Over a minor-suit opening (two diamonds over one diamond, for example), the Michaels Cue-Bid promises good support for both majors. It is like Landy over a minor opening instead of over one notrump, and partner strains to respond by supporting hearts or spades. The cue-bid over a *major* opening promises a two-suiter (at least five of each) including the unbid major suit and an unspecified minor. Partner may support the major directly, or bid two notrump to request the minor. Some partnerships, however, use Michaels Cue-Bids only on three-suited patterns with a singleton or void in the suit bid. Then partner responds as to a takeout double.

An **Astro Cue-Bid** is, again, the direct overcall in opener's suit. Now, however, the takeout bidder has a moderately strong hand (a sound opening bid or better). He has a specific minor-major two-suiter, typically with six cards in the minor, four cards in the major. The cue-bid over one spade or one diamond promises hearts and clubs. Over one club, it promises hearts and diamonds; over one heart, spades and clubs. That is, it indicates hearts unless hearts are bid (then spades); it indicates clubs unless clubs are bid (then diamonds).

A **California Cue-Bid** or **West Coast Cue-Bid** is unrelated to the ones above. This is a bid in the enemy suit, but later in the auction instead of directly over the opening. It asks partner to bid notrump if he has a stopper in that suit.

THE UNUSUAL NOTRUMP

The **Unusual Notrump** is a notrump overcall used as a request for takeout, normally into a minor suit. The overcall is defined as "unusual" in three cases: (1) if made by a passed hand; (2) if made directly over an enemy notrump bid; (3) if made after the opponents have shown great strength. A fourth notrump overcall is commonly deemed to be unusual: (4) the *jump* overcall of two notrump directly over the opening bid. West's overcall below is *not* the unusual notrump:

NORTH	EAST	SOUTH	WEST
1 ♠	Pass	2 ♠	2 NT

However, if West had passed originally, the overcall *would* be unusual (he could not have a powerful balanced hand). If South's response had been *one notrump*, the overcall would be unusual (West would double to show power). If North had passed and South had *opened* two spades as a forcing two-bid, the overcall would be unusual (West would not want to play in notrump against such power); but if the two-bid were *weak*, the overcall would be natural. Finally, if North had passed and South had opened *one* spade, the overcall would be treated by many partnerships as unusual (West would overcall *one* notrump with a strong balanced hand, or double and then bid two notrump with even greater power).

This convention describes a hand with at least ten cards in the minors, normally at least five in each; it is exactly equivalent, both in strength and distribution, to an overcall in both minor suits simultaneously. Responder behaves as if partner had bid both suits. That is, he takes a preference at the cheapest level (even, conceivably, with a doubleton) if he has few useful values; he gives a *jump preference* if he would have raised either suit voluntarily.

Many partnerships use the unusual notrump as a request for unbid suits. If the opponents have bid hearts and clubs, the takeout is for spades and diamonds. If the opponents have bid only diamonds, the unusual notrump calls for hearts and clubs—the two lowest-ranking unbid suits.

When the opponents use this convention against you, remember that the "general principles" discussed earlier provide you with two different defenses. Suppose that your partner opens one heart and your right-hand opponent bids two notrump for the minors. Any time you hold more than your share of high cards (10 points or so) you *double*. Other actions *deny* the strength to double: three hearts is a normal raise; four hearts is based on strong distribution; three spades shows a powerful suit but is nonforcing (since you did not double). And a special bid is available —you can "cue-bid" one of the minors. This should show interest in *both* majors, typically five spades and three hearts; again it denies great strength because you failed to double. The same sort of defense should be used against Michaels or Astro Cue-Bids.

DRURY

The **Drury** convention is a simple device, used, in self-protection, by partnerships prone to light opening bids in third or fourth position. After a major-suit opening, responder, who has previously passed, may bid *two clubs* as an artificial force. Opener will then rebid *two diamonds* (without relation to his diamond holding) if his opening was subminimum or marginal; any other rebid (even the minimum rebid of his major suit) indicates a sound opening, an interest in game opposite a passed hand. Responder, to use Drury, will typically hold a 10-to-12-point hand with three or four cards in opener's major. If responder has, unluckily, a normal club response, he will "rebid" clubs over the reply. If opener has a sound opening with diamonds as his second suit, he will reply two diamonds but bid again when responder signs off. Drury is normally used only in uncontested auctions; in competition, a club response is natural.

When your opponents announce Drury on their convention card, you may draw the inference that they frequently open light hands opposite a passed partner. In defense, I suggest a variation from the general principles. Double the Drury two-club response to show an ordinary passed-hand takeout double of opener's major suit; that is, you promise length not only in clubs but in the two unbid suits as well. However, the double of the artificial two-diamond reply should show only diamonds—a diamond *suit*, not quite good enough for an overcall, but with which you would welcome a three-diamond bid from partner.

BLACKWOOD, GERBER AND COMPANY

All partnerships are assumed to be using some slam convention to check on aces; if no announcement is made, this is everyday **Blackwood.** One variation which you may encounter is **Roman Blackwood.** Here, the responses are different. Five clubs, in reply to four notrump, shows no aces or *three* aces; five diamonds shows one ace or *four.* To show *two* aces, and this is the point of the convention, responder has a choice of two bids—five hearts, five spades—and can give partner a clue as to which aces they are. Five *hearts* shows two aces of the same color (both red, both black) or of the same rank (both major, both minor). Five spades shows two unmatched aces (hearts-clubs or spades-diamonds). Kings are shown, over five notrump, according to the same schedule.

In **Gerber,** the bid of *four clubs* is the ace-asking convention; responses are by steps, as to Blackwood, but, obviously, each suit now shows one ace fewer than in Blackwood (hearts means *one* ace, not two). If your opponents check the Gerber box in the section of their convention card devoted to notrump bidding, they are likely to use both Blackwood *and* Gerber. Four clubs is Gerber only when four notrump would be construed as a natural invitational raise of a notrump bid. These players most often use *five clubs* as the inquiry for kings, after four clubs has asked for aces. In contrast, if your opponents write "Gerber" on the back of their convention card, they use four clubs *in place of* four notrump to ask for aces. Nearly *all* their four-club bids are conventional. And they subsequently ask for kings by bidding the cheapest unbid suit over partner's reply to four clubs.

Gerber and Stayman may clash after an opening (or rebid, following an artificial two-club opening) of three notrump. One popular solution is to use *four clubs* as Stayman, *four diamonds* as Gerber. Another difficulty occurs after a *two*-notrump opening: most partnerships use a direct four clubs as Gerber; many also use three clubs (Stayman) followed by four clubs as Gerber—how can responder show clubs? My own practice is to treat the direct jump to four clubs as natural, showing a strong hand with clubs. To use Gerber, I must first bid three clubs (Stayman) and then bid four clubs.

The **San Francisco** convention shows both aces and kings simultaneously in answer to four notrump. Aces are counted as 3 points each, kings as 1 point. With fewer than 3 points, the response is five *clubs;* with 3 points, it is five *diamonds;* with 4 points, five *hearts;* and so on up the line. However, when four notrump is bid by a player who has opened with a strong two-bid, the response of five diamonds shows only 1 point, and the scale goes on from there.

RESPONSIVE AND NEGATIVE DOUBLES

A **responsive double** is a conventional reply to a takeout double. The auction below is typical:

NORTH	EAST	SOUTH	WEST
1 ♡	Double	2 ♡	Double

West's double, normally for penalties, is for *takeout* if this convention is employed. Ordinarily, West's hand, for the auction above, would contain a scattered 7 to 11 points with three cards in spades (if West had *four* spades, he would probably bid them himself). However, if East answers the double by bidding spades and West then takes out to clubs, West holds both clubs and diamonds. The original takeout doubler responds to the responsive double by bidding his best suit, or by jumping (or cue-bidding) if he has maximum values. The double is "responsive" only after a *raise;* if South, in the auction above, had bid two *diamonds*, West's double would be for penalties.

The **negative double,** or **Sputnik** as it is somtimes called, is a conventional reply to an opening bid. For example:

NORTH	EAST	SOUTH	WEST
1 ♠	2 ◇	Double	

South's double is for *takeout,* not for penalties, if this convention is in use. South promises length in hearts and clubs, the unbid suits, but denies strength for a free bid at the level required (for the auction above, South is likely to have about 6 to 10 points). North will respond to the double by supporting hearts or clubs, by rebidding a long spade suit, by bidding notrump, or, conceivably, by passing with strong diamonds. Any jump response is merely invitational; North must cue-bid in order to force.

Some partnerships play the negative double only after spade overcalls of minor-suit opening bids. In this restricted use, the double specifically promises four *hearts;* it says nothing about the unbid minor, and it is not rigidly limited in strength.

Both conventional doubles are usually played at lower levels only, and the point at which the double becomes for penalties is agreed to and announced. A convention card might read, "Negative doubles through three hearts; responsive doubles through three spades." This means that the double of an overcall of three spades and higher is for penalties; the double of a preemptive raise to four clubs and higher, following a takeout double, is for penalties.

When either convention is used against you, treat "Redouble" as the only strength-showing call. All other actions, even jumps, are predicated on distributional values and are nonforcing. After a negative double, the preemptive jump raise of partner's overcall can be an effective measure.

When your opponents announce negative doubles, you can afford to overcall a trifle more freely than you normally do, since your right-hand opponent cannot make an immediate penalty double. There *is* a mechanism to catch you: your opponent passes with a normal penalty double; opener balances with a takeout double, and responder converts it by passing again. However, responder usually has only a tentative penalty double and so is reluctant to pass for penalties before consulting partner; the fact is that negative doublers are not well placed to punish audacious overcalls. Another related feature of your opponents' bidding is this: opener, when an overcall is passed around to him, is under considerable pressure to bid again—after all, his partner may be lying in the bushes with a penalty double. Therefore, when *your* partner overcalls, you may occasionally pass with a strong defensive hand, intending to double the enemy when they reopen.

ROMAN TWO DIAMONDS

The **Roman Two Diamonds** is an artificial, forcing opening bid. It describes a three-suited hand (4-4-4-1 or 5-4-4) with 17 points or more in high cards. The response of two notrump is positive and game forcing; opener will then bid his singleton or void, and responder will place the contract. A *suit* response is natural, weak and nonforcing. Opener may raise if he has maximum values, and he will, of course, run to the next-higher suit if partner has picked his singleton or void.

The **Miles Two Diamonds** is a variation in which the negative response to two diamonds is *two hearts*. Opener rebids in his short suit, and responder places the contract.

If your opponents use this convention, stay out of the auction and lead trumps when it is over.

TWO CLUBS FORCING

The use of *two clubs* as an artificial, strong, forcing opening bid is common to many different methods. This convention liberates the other two-bids for the special uses which we will examine under "Treatments." This opening bid is not descriptive; opener merely proclaims that he has a hand of enormous power. It is the *rebid* that defines the hand: if in a suit, a "forcing two-bid" with length in that suit; if in notrump, a balanced powerhouse of 23 to 24 points (2 notrump) or 25 to 26 points (3 notrump).

Two diamonds is used as an artificial negative response, equivalent to two notrump in answer to a natural forcing two-bid. (This use of the next-higher suit as a negative response is called the **Herbert convention** when employed as a response to natural two-bids or to takeout doubles.) Two notrump is a positive response based on scattered values; suit responses other than two diamonds are natural and positive (*three* diamonds is the positive response in diamonds). However, some partnerships use an almost automatic two-diamond response; then a positive response promises an exceptionally strong suit. Other partnerships may announce **step responses** to two clubs; then the response is artificial, showing by "steps" (as in the San Francisco convention, for example) how many aces and kings responder holds. Still others may show aces (individually) over two clubs.

The two-club convention affects the two-notrump opening bid, since opener will first bid two clubs and then rebid two notrump (nonforcing) with 23 or 24 points, and possibly with a well-bolstered 22 as well. Thus, the *opening* of two notrump is weaker than standard: from a maximum of 22 points down to a hefty 20.

Similarly, the *three*-notrump opening bid is released for other duty. Some partnerships use **Gambling Three Notrump openings** (**Acol Three Notrump** is the same thing). This opening bid announces a long, solid suit, almost invariably a minor, with little more than a king or queen on the side. Responder will pass if he has a few scattered high cards; with weak hands he will run to four clubs and opener will pass or correct to his suit. Other partnerships use the three-notrump opening to describe a long minor suit in a *strong* hand, a hand with a point count for *two* notrump but with the makings of nine tricks. Still others open three notrump with balanced hands of 27 or 28 points. Only the first of these treatments (Gambling Three

Notrump) is customarily announced, so it is well to ask questions if the bid comes up.

When your opponents open with two clubs, you should not automatically stay out of the auction. Particularly if you are nonvulnerable against vulnerable opponents, competition may be handsomely rewarded. Opener has not yet described his hand, so jamming tactics can be most effective. My recommendations for defense against the artificial one-club opening (see p. 119) apply here as well.

In defending against the Gambling Three Notrump, you may care to adopt a variety of Ripstra. Bid four in a minor (the minor suit which you think opener does *not* have) for takeout into a major. Partner should usually bid hearts or spades, but he may, in dire emergency, pass. Double the opening with a strong balanced hand, suitable to defense. And on lead against this three-notrump opening, tend to open an ace if you have one, in order to take a look at dummy.

TREATMENTS

The bids which will be described in this section are mostly "natural," in the sense that they promise length in the bid suit, although you may find some of them bizarre. Generally, the regulations which govern the use of treatments are more lenient than those for conventions; the A.C.B.L. allows you more scope for eccentricity. If you deem it wise to have your one-notrump opening promise 19 to 21 points, or to open only *six*-card majors, or to play that a double-jump shift guarantees a solid suit, no one will stop you from indulging your fancy. The principal requirements are that your agreement must be one which can be fully explained in a few words, and that these few words must be written on your convention card.

TWO-BIDS, WEAK AND STRONG

In the absence of any announcement, you may assume that your opponents' opening two-bids are natural and game-forcing. However, if they play Two Clubs Forcing be sure that you look to see what their *other* two-bids mean.

The **weak two-bid** is the usual companion of the forcing two-club opening. Here, the opening bid of two diamonds, two hearts or two spades is semipreemptive, describing a hand with five to seven winners but without either the high-card content of a one-bid or the freakish distribution of a three-bid. Here is an example hand with which every weak-two-bidder in the world would open two spades:

♠ K Q J 9 6 4   ♡ 5 2   ◇ K 7 3   ♣ 8 4

It would be impossible, however, to produce unanimous agreement about any (even slightly) different hand. For instance, if the *ace* of diamonds were substituted for the king, many would open *one* spade but most would still open two. If the spade *queen* were replaced by the deuce, some would pass, deeming the suit too weak, while as many others would be undeterred. Even if the spade *king* were similarly exchanged for a low card, some brave souls would open a nonvulnerable two-bid. Perhaps because of this wide variation, the A.C.B.L. has established an inviolable rule that weak two-bids must contain between 6 and 12 points, no more and no less (but this rule, with its broad range, accomplishes little; it serves merely to annoy the experts who resent being told how to bid). A vague description of a weak two-bid, which would apply to almost any style, is this: a "good" six-card suit (occasionally a very strong five-card suit, very rarely a seven-card suit) in a hand that has a "little" defensive strength (usually one or two tricks).

Responses to weak two-bids vary also, but they are announced. The single raise is always preemptive, the two-notrump response is always forcing. However, some partnerships use two notrump as the *only* forcing response; a new suit response is in the nature of a rescue bid and requests opener to pass. In other partnerships, a new suit response is forcing (except by a passed hand, of course); it may be a slam try, a feeler for notrump, a legitimate suit or an out-and-out psychic. Always look to see which responses your opponents use, even when no such response is made, for this will be a clue to their style: those who use two-notrump-only-force are more inclined to open in shabby suits than are the new-suit-forcing group (who do not want to be rescued). Opener's rebid over the two-notrump response is commonly the same for both factions. He will show a side feature, or rebid his suit with a minimum or raise notrump with a solid suit. However, you may run into **Ogust rebids:** three *clubs* and three *diamonds* show a shabby suit with a minimum or a maximum respectively; the rebid of the suit shows minimum strength but a husky suit; three notrump shows a solid suit.

Defend against weak two-bids in hearts or diamonds much as you do against one-bids; your opponent is a little weaker, but you are up a little higher—it comes out about even. However, defend against a two-*spade* opening as you customarily do against *three*-bids .Watch out for psychic responses if your opponents use new-suits-forcing. The double of such a response should be for *penalties;* in contrast, if two notrump is the only force, double a new suit response for *takeout.*

Acol Two-Bids are an alternate use of two diamonds, two hearts and two spades when two clubs is artificial. These are natural *strong* bids, but are forcing only for one round, not to game. Opener typically has an eight- or nine-winner hand with a powerful suit. Conceivably, he has two strong suits; in this case, he may intend to force to game later, preferring the natural opening bid to two clubs for tactical reasons. The negative response is two notrump; any other response is positive, promising high-card values, and forcing to game. In general, partnerships using Acol Two-Bids tend to lower their minimum requirements for *one*-bids.

Intermediate Two-Bids are much the same as Acol Two-Bids, but have slightly lower limits. Often they are played as invitational, rather than as forcing for one round. Responses are as to Acol Two-Bids.

ONE NOTRUMP OPENING BIDS

The A.C.B.L. rule is that all partnerships must announce the range of their one-notrump opening bids, and that the spread must be no greater than 3 points (or four *levels:* 15, 16, 17, 18). The most common point ranges announced are, of course, "15 to 17," "15 to 18," and "16 to 18"—the normal **strong notrump.** There is actually even less difference between these ranges than meets the eye, for most players who announce "16 to 18" will occasionally open with 15, and those who announce "15 to 18" rarely open with 18 (however, the "16-to-18" players frequently *do* open 18-point hands with one notrump). Your normal defensive measures should be used against these ranges without distinction, and you should probably treat the rare "14-to-16" range in the same fashion.

The **weak notrump** is quite different. The usual ranges announced—"11 to 14," "12 to 14," "12 to 15"—are, again, virtually identical in practice. The 11-point hands are opened only seldom (nonvulnerable, with 3 quick tricks or with a strong five-card suit); even 12-point hands are frequently passed, when vulnerability is unfavorable or when they are overloaded with queens and jacks; 15-point hands are rarely opened one notrump (those that are, bear a family resemblance to the 12-point hands which are passed). Almost any weak notrump opening describes a hand with which a Standard bidder, using "15 to 18," would open in a suit and rebid one notrump.

There are, however, two different schools among weak notrumpers. One group will use this opening only with ideal notrump hands (stoppers, tenace positions, etc.), feeling free to open a 13- or 14-point balanced hand with a *suit* bid if it has a flaw. The other group (Kaplan-Shein-wold players, for example) open virtually *all* minimum balanced hands with one notrump; their partners (and their opponents) can draw the inference that they have either a *strong* or an *unbalanced* hand when they open, instead, in a suit. Both schools use the *rebid* of one notrump, particularly after a minor-suit opening, to promise 15 points or more, but their other rebids differ considerably. You can get a strong clue to your opponents' style by noticing whether or not they open four-card majors. If they *do*, they probably pick and choose their notrump openings; but if they play Five-Card Majors, they are likely to open almost all of their minimum balanced hands with one notrump.

Your approach to defense against the *weak* notrump opening must be different from that against *strong* notrump. Primarily, this is because your objective has changed —you are no longer merely competing, harassing the enemy on a hand that almost surely belongs to *them;* instead, *your* side will own the hand perhaps one-third of the time, and you may even have a game. You should have three principal defensive weapons: the penalty double, a conventional bid for takeout and the overcall.

Sitting over the notrump opening, double for penalties with either of two types of hand: a balanced hand of 15 points or more, or a hand which contains a long, easily established suit and a side entry. (Partner should pass your double with all balanced hands, taking out only with wild distribution. All subsequent doubles of escape suits should be for penalties.) If you have good support for the major suits, prefer to use your takeout convention, Landy for example, instead of the double—even when you are very strong; you may not defeat one notrump doubled enough to compensate for what *you* could have made. (Partner should be much more apt to *jump* in response, if he has suitable values, than after a strong notrump; and you may raise a nonjump response when you have unusual strength.) When you have a strong hand with a long broken suit, *jump-overcall* to invite game. The simple overcall is limited by your failure to choose one of the stronger actions; it should be predicated on unbalanced distribution, not great high-card power. Overcall freely when your pattern is wild (6-4-2-1, 5-5-2-1) but pass flat hands (5-3-3-2) which are too weak for the double. (Partner should treat your overcalls as semipreemptive, and pass unless he has a sound opening bid or better.)

In balancing position (one notrump on your *left,* passed around to you), double only with the powerful high-card hand. If responder bids two clubs before you have a chance to double, double *that;* this should not show *clubs,* as it would after a strong notrump. Jump-overcall rather than double when you hold a strong suit as well as high point count; the difference is that you are not on lead. For the same reason, use the simple overcall even without wild shape when your suit is very good—partner is about to lead some foolish suit of his own.

The only really extraordinary notrump opening which you are likely to encounter is the **Woodson Two-Way Notrump.** Here the opening shows *either* 10 to 12 points *or* 16 to 18 points. (This treatment has a dispensation from the A.C.B.L. with respect to the "four levels" rule.) Obviously, the opening is most often 10 to 12, but responder must bid with 8 points—he usually bids *two clubs*. Now, opener answers *two diamonds* or *two hearts* (natural) with 10 to 12; any other response shows 16 to 18.

Defend as against weak notrump. However, be alert to opportunities for later penalty doubles, after the two-club artificial response elicits a minimum reply.

JUMP OVERCALLS

Strong jump overcalls promise about an ace more than a minimum opening bid, with a magnificent suit to boot. The typical strong jump overcall is made on a hand with which, if you were dealer, you would open the bidding and then jump-rebid in your long suit. The bid is not forcing. However, partner should strain to find a response (usually a raise, since the jump overcaller is not likely to be interested in a new suit—that is why he did not double) if he would have responded to an opening bid.

Intermediate jump overcalls describe the sort of hand with which, if you were dealer, you would open the bidding and then rebid your suit twice without jumping—a minimum opening with a solid or semisolid suit. Responses are natural; responder needs just under an opening bid of his own (or strong distributional support) to think of game.

Preemptive jump overcalls are made with hands that would call for a pass (or, at best, a weak two-bid) if the opponent had not opened. Let me illustrate all three varieties of jump overcall with a series of examples—suppose that your right-hand opponent opens with one club, and you are considering a jump to two spades with one of these hands:

(1)	♠ A K Q J 8 4	♡ A 6	◇ A Q J 7	♣ 2
(2)	♠ K Q J 8 6 4 2	♡ A 6	◇ 7	♣ K Q 2
(3)	♠ A K Q 8 4 2	♡ A 6 3	◇ 7 2	♣ 8 2
(4)	♠ K Q J 10 4 2	♡ 6 3	◇ A Q 7	♣ 8 2
(5)	♠ A Q J 10 8 4	♡ Q 6	◇ Q 7 2	♣ 8 2
(6)	♠ K Q J 8 6 4	♡ 6 3	◇ J 7 5 2	♣ 2
(7)	♠ Q J 10 6 4 2	♡ 6 3	◇ 7 5 2	♣ 8 2

Example (1) is too strong for even a strong jump overcall; it calls for a cue-bid. Hand (2), however, is a typical strong jump. Hand (3) is a trifle weak for a strong jump, a trifle strong for an intermediate jump; either school might jump anyway, but would more likely double. Example (4) is a typical intermediate jump. With hand (5), the intermediate school would feel a little weak, the preemptive school a bit strong; either might well jump, but might rather bid *one* spade instead. Example (6) is a typical preemptive jump. Example (7) would be passed by most; only a particularly radical preemptive jumper in one of his weaker moments would bid two spades.

The usual response to the preemptive jump overcall is to pass. However, responder will raise or jump-raise partner's suit if he has a fit. The single raise is a "barricade" bid, not a game try; the jump to game is often preemptive also, a premature sacrifice, but may of course be made with a strong hand. New suit responses are rare; they are normally played as forcing (by an unpassed hand).

A good case can be made for using the negative double (see p. 130) over your opponents' strong or intermediate jump overcalls, since you will seldom want to double for penalties—the enemy suit is too powerful. In addition, it is probably right to play that a new suit by responder, bid over a *strong* jump overcall, is nonforcing.

Preemptive jump overcalls can present you with nasty problems. Responder often has a decent hand, but not enough strength for a free bid at the required level. If he bids, he will get too high; if he passes, the hand may be stolen from him when opener passes also; and if opener reopens with sketchy values, responder may decide to make a bid to show that he has something, and this may get the partnership too high again. My recommendation is for opener to make an arbitrary assumption that responder holds about 6 to 8 points for his pass over a preemptive jump overcall. If this is enough for safety at the required level, opener will bid again; if this is all that responder holds, he will do nothing violent. And if responder does *not* have his points, he owes opener an apology.

JUMP-SHIFT RESPONSES

If no announcement is made on their convention card, your opponents use **strong jump shifts** (in this sense, "jump shift" means responder's jump in a new suit over an opening bid of one in a suit). There are many differing partnership styles in jump shifts. Some restrict the bid to monstrously powerful hands of 19 points or more; others regard it as merely a mild slam suggestion which can be made with 15 points. Or the jump shift can be used to promise specific values: a completely solid suit, or a fit with opener's suit, for example. And when the jump shift is made by a passed hand, some play it as a force, implying a fit with opener, while others deem it merely an invitation based on a maximum passed hand and a good suit. However, you will almost never consider entering the auction over an enemy jump shift, so you can wait until the bidding is over and then ask any material questions.

Occasionally, though, you will encounter pairs who announce **weak jump-shift responses.** *Their* jump shift promises a six-card suit (or, rarely, a good five-card suit) and little more. This preemptive jump is made with the sort of hand with which you would sign off at two of a suit if your partner opened with a strong notrump. Thus, opener must be unusually powerful (or must have a good fit) in order to try for game. Usually he will pass, or rescue with another suit. Weak jump-shift responses are usually understood to include responses to a first- or second-hand opening—not jumps by a passed hand.

There are variations in which jump shifts are weak only when an overcall intervenes (they are *commonly* played as weak over an intervening double). Some play jump responses as weak when made by a passed hand. And there are many varieties of suit jumps by responder over a one-notrump opening (preemptive, invitational, weak in minors but strong in majors, etc.). These are normally listed separately under notrump bidding on the convention card; they are not jump shifts.

RESPONDER'S RAISES

The Standard treatment of responder's raises of opener's suit, which requires no announcement on the convention card, is as follows: The *jump* (one diamond–three diamonds), by an unpassed hand, is forcing to game and promises 12–13 points or more. The *single* raise (one heart–two hearts) is mildly discouraging, roughly within the range of 5 to 10 points. Over this single raise, opener will pass with minimum values, jump to game with maximum values; with intermediate strength, opener will try for game in either of two ways: by bidding the new suit (a forcing *trial bid*) in which he most needs help; or by reraising in his own suit (or bidding two notrump) if maximum values *anywhere* in responder's hand will be useful.

A common variation, which must be announced, is **preemptive reraises.** Here, if opener bids *one heart*, responder raises to *two hearts*, and opener then rebids *three hearts*, responder MUST pass. Opener is preempting with a minimum unbalanced hand anticipating reopening action by his opponents. If opener were interested in game, he would employ a trial bid (or two notrump) instead of the reraise.

A different sort of trial bid is one called the **short-suit game try.** Here if opener rebids in a new suit after a single raise, he needs values in responder's hand *outside* this suit. Typically, opener holds a void or singleton (rarely, a small doubleton) in the suit of his trial bid.

Limit raises is the usual announcement for the treatment in which the *jump raise* is invitational rather than forcing. The single raise has a top limit of 8 or 9 points; the jump raise takes over from there, promising 10 (occasionally, a magnificent 9) to 12 points. With 13 points or more, responder will *not* jump-raise, but what he *will* do is a matter for individual agreement: in most partnerships, responder will bid a new suit, then force with a delayed jump raise at his second turn; in some partnerships, a conventional bid is set aside for the forcing raise (see below); in a few partnerships, the jump to *four* (in a major) is used as stronger than the jump to *three*. The limit jump raise to three is exactly equivalent to the normal jump raise by a *passed hand;* opener will go on to game only if he holds slightly more than minimum values. Some partnerships use limit raises in the majors only, or in the minors only; this is, of course, announced on the convention card.

Several devices are currently in use as adjuncts to the limit jump raise in a major suit, which act as *forcing* raises. In one, the response of *three notrump* to a major-suit opening bid is artificial and forcing, promising four-card support for opener's suit. In a different method, the **Swiss convention,** the responses of *four clubs* and *four* *diamonds* are both used to show support for opener's major; four diamonds is stronger than four clubs, the usual distinction being that four diamonds promises (and four clubs denies) three first-round controls or two first-round controls plus the king of trumps. Over any of these artificial responses, opener rebids exactly as he would over a standard forcing raise, bidding game in his suit with a minimum or making a slam try with extra strength.

Inverted minor-suit raises is a treatment quite different from **limit raise in minors.** In inverted raises, the single raise (one diamond–two diamonds) is *strong*, while the jump raise (one diamond–three diamonds) is *preemptive*. This single raise is forcing for one round with an approximate range of from 9 or 10 up to 16 points. (That is, it embraces both the limit jump raise and the forcing jump raise.) Over it, opener tends to rebid in notrump with even distribution, *two* notrump with a minimum, *three* notrump with extra values; opener, with unbalanced distribution, will always reraise to show minimum values, and will bid a new suit (often, but not always, a long side suit) to suggest extra strength. The jump raise is equivalent in strength to a normal single raise, but most often contains five trumps and uneven pattern; the alternative weak response of one notrump is preferred for hands with four trumps and more balanced distribution. Over the jump raise, opener will pass unless his hand is unusually powerful.

Raises after an intervening takeout double are treated by virtually all partnerships as preemptive, without regard to the methods employed for uncontested auctions. Many, though, use the jump to *two notrump* (one heart–double–two notrump) to describe a limit jump raise in opener's suit.

PSYCHIC OPENING BIDS

If your opponents have checked the box on their convention card which says "Frequent Psychics," they tend to open the bidding, as a matter of system, whenever they hold unusually weak hands—perhaps on the order of once or twice a session. Then it is a fair inference to draw that your opponent has a smattering of high cards when he passes in first or second seat nonvulnerable. In contrast, those who check "Occasional Psychics" mean that their bidding methods allow opener to give way to an irresistible impulse now and again, but that this is irregular and unexpected—it happens not more than once in two or three sessions. Finally, the opponents who check nothing presumably have agreed never to psyche.

The typical old-fashioned, red-blooded psycher likes to bid the suit that is most likely to be the enemy's—his psychic one-spade opening is made with a *short suit*, such as ten-doubleton. However, there is a modern effete school (Roth-Stone, Kaplan-Sheinwold players and others) who use the psychic opening in a long suit; it is a descriptive bid. Their one-spade opening would typically be five to the K J, or four to the Q J 10. Partner may well raise opener's suit even after the psychic has been exposed, and partner will tend to lead that suit on defense.

Controlled psychics are used only by the long-suit school. Here, some response—usually the jump shift—is designated as a "control" against a possible psychic opening. If opener has psyched, he must not pass but, instead, must make a specific rebid: the cheapest number of notrump in some partnerships; the next-higher suit in others; the rebid of his original suit; either notrump or the original suit, whichever is cheaper. In any case, opener promises a legitimate bid if he selects some rebid other than the one used in his partnership to denote a psychic.

The best defense against psychics is probably to bid normally, treating the opening as legitimate until it is proven otherwise. However, against frequent short-suit psychics you may care to play that all bids in opener's suit are natural, not cue-bids.

FIVE-CARD MAJORS

Many of your opponents will announce that they do not open four-card majors in first or second seat (and, sometimes, in *any* position). Actually, this is not so great a divergence from Standard bidding as is popularly supposed. After all, *everybody's* major openings usually are five-card suits or longer: you are most often dealt a long suit; with two four-card suits, you probably would bid the minor unless the suits were touching, and even *then* if the major were weak; with only one four-card suit, you tend to open in notrump or in a short minor. What is more, players who

announce that they play Five-Card Majors will occasionally violate their system and open in a strong four-card
suit. Consider these three hands:

(1)	♠ K J 7 2	♡ 8 5	◇ A Q 4	♣ K 8 4 3
(2)	♠ 2	♡ A K Q 5	◇ K 7 6 3 2	♣ J 8 6
(3)	♠ A 6 4	♡ K Q 7 2	◇ K J 5 3	♣ 1 0 2

Hand (1) would be opened one club by most four-card
majorites; hand (2) would be opened one heart by most
Five-Card Major players; only in hand (3) would the difference show up, one school opening one heart, the other
one diamond.

The Five-Card Major treatment creates a slight difference in responses. Responder is very free to raise a major
with three-card support; if he responds one notrump, he
is unlikely to hold more than two cards in partner's suit.
Minor-suit raises are given much more reluctantly—almost
never with three cards, more often with five than with
four cards. One responder is more prone than in Standard
to bid a weak four-card major in reply to a minor-suit opening. Therefore, opener is less likely than usual to raise this
major-suit response with only three-card support. However, opener's rebids after a *major* opening are hardly affected at all. If he rebids his major over a two-level
response, he does *not* promise a six-card suit; he is simply
limiting his hand.

Many Five-Card Major partnerships play **One Notrump
Forcing**; that is, opener must not pass the response of one
notrump. Instead, he rebids his major if it is a six-carder
or an unusually powerful five-carder. (*This* is the auction
in which a rebid tends to show six cards; but it does in
Standard, also.) Failing this, he bids a side four-card suit.
And if he has no other suit (with 5–3–3–2 shape), he bids
his lower-ranking three-card suit. Thus, in:

OPENER	RESPONDER
1 ♠	1 NT
2 ♣	

opener is as likely as not to have a three-card club suit;
had he rebid two *diamonds,* it could possibly be a three-

card suit, but is probably four cards long. What sort of hand will responder have to bid one notrump forcing? Exactly the sort of hand, usually, with which *you* would bid one notrump *nonforcing*. Conceivably, he may have as much as 11 points, but this is rare. Normally, what is different is not the response of one notrump itself, but merely that opener must bid over it.

No special method of defense is necessary against Five-Card Majors. However, keep in mind the three situations in which weak or short suits are often bid: the major-suit response to a minor opening; the minor-suit rebid by opener after a forcing notrump response; the minor-suit opening itself, which is rather more often than in Standard made in a weak three-card suit. Some players use the overcall in opener's minor as a natural bid instead of a cue-bid, when the opponents announce Five-Card Majors. Remember, though, that a minor opening is far more often a long suit than a short one, so this usage may tempt you into indiscretion.

ONE CLUB FORCING

How to classify the announcement **"One Club Forcing"** which is frequently encountered on the convention cards—as a system, a convention or a treatment—is a difficult decision. It can be any one of the three. The only thing that all One Club Forcing partnerships have in common is that they use the response of *one diamond* as an artificial negative (so *you* should use the overcall of two diamonds, after this response, to show a diamond suit). As to what the one-club bid itself implies, there is no general agreement.

One group uses the one-club opening for all hands of greater than a certain specified count (normally the figure is put somewhere between 15 and 18 points). This is, of course, a system—with all kinds of negative inferences attached to auctions that are *not* started with one club. You have no possibility of learning exactly what the opponents' bidding means, but the odds are that they are not quite sure themselves, so do not worry. Defend as against the Schenken Club (see p. 119).

A second group plays one club as a force in order to cater to strong hands of the type of Acol Two-Bids. If opener's rebid is a jump shift, he describes such a hand;

his second suit is his long one, and his strength is just under that of a forcing two-bid. But if opener's rebid is normal, so is his one-club opening. You need no special defense here, since the conventional use of one club is rare and has little limiting effect on other auctions.

The largest group uses One Club Forcing as an adjunct to Five-Card Majors. It is a short club which has been cut *so* short that it no longer has any relationship to clubs. These players tend to bid one club whenever their hand does not qualify for either a major-suit or a one-notrump opening—often with a doubleton club, conceivably even with a singleton. Here, you should treat your overcall of two clubs as natural, showing clubs.

By far the most important factor in defense against One Club Forcing is discovering which group your opponents belong to. Whenever you see this announcement on their card, ask a series of questions before the auction begins. I suggest these three: What sort of hand do you open with one club when you are short in clubs? Does the failure to open one club limit your *other* opening bids in any way? What do you require to open with *one diamond?* (This question about diamonds is quite necessary. If your opponents play Five-Card Majors and require at least four cards for one diamond, they open two-card club suits. You may even run into a sect that requires *five* cards for one diamond; *they* may have to open one club with a singleton.)

You will find that the more you know about your opponents' bidding the better your scores will be. And the better your scores, the more fun you will have playing the wonderful game of duplicate bridge.

INDEX OF SYSTEMS, CONVENTIONS
AND TREATMENTS

ABOUT THE AUTHOR

EDGAR KAPLAN, who lives in New York City, is the co-owner of the famous Card School at 575 Park Avenue. Captain of the 1964 and 1966 International team, he is a Life Master and has won almost every honor in the game, including the Vanderbilt Cup and the Masters Individual. Mr. Kaplan is the co-author with Alfred Sheinwold of *How to Play Winning Bridge,* and is the author of Bantam's *Winning Contract Bridge Complete, The Complete Italian System of Winning Bridge* and *Competitive Bidding in Modern Bridge.* He is currently U.S. Open Pairs champion, Mixed Pairs champion and champion of the U.S. Men's Team of Four.